Parenting from the Trenches

Parenting from the Trenches

✦

Anecdotes from the Front Lines of Child Rearing

Julie Butler Evans

iUniverse, Inc.
New York Bloomington

Parenting from the Trenches
Anecdotes from the Front Lines
of Child Rearing

iUniverse books may be ordered through booksellers or by contacting:

iUniverse
1663 Liberty Drive
Bloomington, IN 47403
www.iuniverse.com
1-800-Authors (1-800-288-4677)

ISBN: 978-0-595-48895-7 (pbk)
ISBN: 978-0-595-60886-7 (ebk)

Printed in the United States of America

To Blake, Kenny, Janet and Jack.

Contents

ACKNOWLEDGEMENTS

Above all others, I thank my amazing and amusing kids for their ongoing and bottomless love, inspiration, patience and bravery. Having your peccadilloes (as well as your virtues) published for the entire world to see can't always be easy. I appreciate the 99-percent grace you often show regarding that. So much gratitude goes to Jon Evans for your love and support, for financing this endeavor, and for your own bemused tolerance of my various column topics. Many thanks to my editor John Kovach at *The New Canaan Advertiser* for hiring me in the first place to write "Parenting from the Trenches," and for allowing me to put said columns together into this book. Last, but hardly least, I would literally be nowhere had it not been for Holly and Roger Butler, my parents. They taught me about humor in the face of adversity, and that it's easier to be a parent if you keep the kid in you alive.

AUTHOR'S NOTE

When I was the editor of *Connecticut County Kids,* I had a welcoming note in every issue which carried within tales about the high jinks of my children; first just two, then three and finally four kids. Readers seemed to enjoy those bits and followed my children's progress and foibles for 10 years. When I was approached to write a similar column for our local newspaper in 2004, I was thrilled and honored. Topics about parenting and children are never hard to come by in a house with four children, and it is my hope that the columns both amuse and inspire as that has always been my goal.

The job of being a parent offers a multitude of challenges. It is rewarding, frustrating, fascinating. It is touched by enormous love, and occasionally, enormous heartache. Being able to share all of that with other parents has been therapeutic and I feel blessed to be able to do it. I am far from an expert; I'm just another "bozo" mom on the bus. And in the end, I thoroughly enjoy the ride.

Come on into the trenches with me—we can dodge all these bullets together!

"Children aren't happy with nothing to ignore,
And that's what parents were created for."

Ogden Nash

1
BY WAY OF EXPLANATION

When a Child is in the Sandbox

When I tell people that I have four children between the ages of 8 and 20, they usually respond with a "Wow!" "Yep," I say, "it's never boring." And it isn't. Sometimes it's amusingly not boring, and at other times it is *painfully* not boring. Right now, there is a little less laughter and a tad more fear, because my oldest, Blake, is currently serving in combat with the Marines over in Fallujah, Iraq. So while my other three keep me hopping and/or concerned, my focus has nevertheless shifted. And my days are truly far from dull.

This is Blake's second go round in what we Marine moms fondly call "the sandbox." Although it was very hard emotionally last year during his deployment and our country's push into Iraq, this year is particularly difficult as he is seeing far more combat and danger. But like last year, I am grateful for the responsibility and the distraction of his younger bothers and sister.

Kenny, nearly 19, is in college in Florida, majoring in recording arts. He calls quite a bit and there are care packages to send. Like a lot of college students and teenagers in general, he is pretty self-absorbed, but in a healthy way. He doesn't really come up for air with his classes and studying, and he seems not to follow what his brother is doing a world away from Orlando. Jack is 8, and Janet, 11 next month, and they keep me running with various sports and play-dates and visits downtown. They know that Blake is back in Iraq, but blessedly it is not as in-your-face-every-time-you-turn-on-the-television as it was last spring. Janet especially feels my fear and has her own, too. "Let's get Blake some candy," she will suggest when I pick her up from school. Being helpful makes her feel more in control. Jack is very proud of his big brother, and brought him in for show-and-tell last November just before Thanksgiving. His second grade class has written and drawn notes for Blake. Last year the entire first grade donated an incredible amount of items for a care package. I am *still* sending him stuff from their generosity! My children understand that their brother is truly doing something that only the few choose. And they are proud.

This quote from another Marine mom expresses what I feel perfectly: *"Every week is like a rollercoaster ride that I want to get off. When I read a Marine has been killed and his name has not been released pending notification of kin, restlessness, depression and insomnia rule my life until 24 hours have passed, and the men in dress uniforms have not appeared at my door. I pray constantly they will never come ..."*

When you hold your baby close, remember we mothers of American soldiers held our babies, too. Now our "babies" are putting themselves in harm's way for you.

Kenny believes Blake to be invincible and I suppose that's not an entirely bad idea, especially for a sibling. But as his mother, I know differently. I have been keenly aware of his mortality since birth. All through and way past Blake's infancy I would tiptoe into his room at night, lean over the crib or bunk bed and listen/feel for his breathing. A few times I would actually gently shake him awake just to be certain.

And so it is each morning these days when I tiptoe into our study where the computer lives, and check my email and the news. I'm mentally shaking him to know that he breathes. On some days I can exhale, too, yet on other days, I remain breathless, not only praying for Blake but for boredom as well.

2
A LITTLE OF THIS, A LOT OF THAT

Laughter is what I'm after

Laughter is a great way to connect with your children. It's free, it's relatively easy, it's painless and it begets itself.

Some of my fondest memories of my family of origin are of dinner table laughter fits, the ones that produce uncontrollable tears and giggles. At a point in the meal where things might have been uncomfortably silent, my father would usually beguile my mother, brother and me with funny anecdotes—or even slightly tragic ones—causing us to collapse into laughter. I could be brooding, or my younger brother might be restless, and Dad would say something that started us chuckling. The chuckle would begat a giggle and the giggle begat a belly laugh. Instantly we bonded, grabbing one another's hand or arm, dabbing at our eyes with our napkins. The conversation from there would flow and my parents might actually learn something about us that we had been perhaps loathing to reveal.

I don't want to promote sarcasm or disrespect, although it has been my experience that the occasional self-deprecating remark can turn a sullen child silly. Even a slightly sarcastic teasing makes the cranky kid cackle at him or herself. The age old tactic of admonishing a younger child not to smile—"Do not laugh. You cannot laugh"—always works like a charm on the toddler/preschool set.

Giggle-provoking rituals or routines that I thought worked best when my kids were wee can still incite them to laugh. One such instance happens only in the fall when we are driving in the car. On a windy day, when the gusts cause a funnel of leaves to fly at and around the car, I call it a "whoosh;" it makes my stomach seriously dance and tickle. "Look, mommy! A whoosh," the kids would cry when younger, and I would make all manner of crazy sounds while shouting "Whoosh! Whoosh!" Jack will still point out the random whoosh to me, bless his heart, and my gleeful cry of "Whoosh!" can cause Janet to smile in spite of her adolescent self. Kenny and Blake may roll their 20-something eyes and shake their head in supreme embarrassment, but they are grinning while they do it.

Laughter is of course a salve in the face of death, dying or general bad news. Laughing instead of crying can be just as healing and cathartic.

When my grandfather died in 1989, we held a wake for him. As the family, we of course had to be there at the funeral home next to the casket. Before the mourners gathered, it was just my parents, my brother, me and my granddad's body in the room. It was most uncomfortable. There was an errant bee buzzing above grandpa's reposed body which I chose to fixate upon as it dove around his head. I whispered to my brother to check out the bee and we both began to stifle giggles, two grown children in their 30's. Our parents looked at us in horror. I somehow managed in between giggles to whisper to my mother the whereabouts of the bee before quickly shuffling outside with my brother to the safety of a back porch where we began laughing out loud. Within moments, mom and dad joined us and the four of us hugged and laughed, the tears of grief more real than those for the prankster bee's folly.

And so it goes. A smile can sometimes bridge the gap between trial and tragedy better than a frown. Laughter at oneself, or others or a situation may open up a dialogue between parent and child that had somehow gone missing. And is there nothing more beautiful than your child when he or she is smiling?

Kids and Cleaning: Do They Really Mix?

Although the phrase, "Clean your room!" is uttered by every parent to every child 12 zillion times a day all over cities, towns and villages in all of the 50 states, the idea of cleaning is something that seems to take kids a very long time to understand, let alone follow through on in a meaningful manner.

If you are the fellow parent of a teenager, you know exactly what I mean. "Clean" means shove everything under the bed or into the closet. Even clothes you have just freshly washed, folded and placed onto their unmade beds are thrown willy-nilly into the laundry hamper, rather than placed in dresser drawers. Hand them a can of Pledge and a rag and they will most likely just spray the scent into the air using the rag to circulate the lemon fragrance throughout the room.

"See mom," they say. "I cleaned!" Nice try, kid.

The faulty cleaning gene goes beyond the teenage years, unless of course you are lucky to have a child in the military—as I do—and then they truly understand tightly made beds, mopped floors and clean until they shine toilets.

Last week I traveled to my son Kenny's apartment to offer my cleaning services. Four young men are sharing one bathroom. It was an absolute horror; worse than anything I have ever seen in the way of filthy. The cleaning up literally had me gagging, but the toilet was so disgusting that I didn't dare throw up in it for fear I'd never stop. I relied on bleach fumes to keep my lunch in place. Disinfecting the bathroom was all that I could handle that day.

I left all my cleaning substances and several rolls of paper towels behind with a strong suggestion that Kenny and his cohorts actually use them. More than once a year. I highly doubt I will be making a return cleaning engagement.

When Kenny and Blake were about nine and 10, I would ask them nicely to pick up their toys ands clothes in their bedrooms. After the second request would go unheeded, I took some advice I read somewhere: Simply put everything that was on their floor into a large, plastic trash bag. I wasn't going to throw the bag out. But they didn't know that. I only had to do this about three times before they got the message.

Younger children usually delight in helping mommy and daddy to clean things: Spraying the window cleaner and mopping it up with loads of paper towels. Trying so hard to navigate their sheets and blankets to make their bed. Helping to push the vacuum cleaner over the rug. Yet at some point—usually around kindergarten or first grade—they seem to lose interest. And ability.

Blake began washing his own clothes in about the fifth grade (Kenny was in college before he ever met a washing machine!), and Jack, nine, learned his way around a washer-and-dryer in third grade. I introduced Janet to the vacuum cleaner late this past fall, but she hasn't been especially interested in making another date with the Dyson since.

Because I work at home more these days, I recently let our cleaning woman go.

"What?!" screamed Janet when I told her. "Who is going to clean my room now?" I simply smiled at her while she grimaced, realizing the harsh reality of what my smile meant. And then she quickly recovered.

"Oh good," she said like a princess before closing the door to her bedroom on my Cheshire cat face. "That means you can clean it!"

I'll have the last laugh though: the only princess she will resemble will be Cinderella before the Ball. I'm so wicked. But it's all good, clean fun.

The Passion of the Child

Hell hath no fury like a child scorned.

It is Major League Baseball playoff time, a time of great joy and/or sorrow, peppered with shouts of obscenities or triumph, at least in our house. Both my husband and son, Jack, are rabid Yankee fans, although I question Jack's loyalty when the Yanks are behind; he becomes something altogether different than an adoring admirer when the chips are seemingly down for the Bronx Bombers.

When he was younger, the screams and cries—although explosive in nature—were more along the lines of: "Stupid Yankees! What the *heck*?!" And, now, the 11-year-old younger brother of two older male siblings with questionable vocabularies, substitutes the words "stupid" and "heck" with more colorful terms. This only results in more exasperation when he is properly parentally scolded, while *I* silently curse both the Yankees and my son for losing control of the game.

Jack's buddy, Drew, is a Red Sox enthusiast, and his mom reports that their house is just as tense during games. One time this past summer, Jack went over to Drew's house to watch a Yankees-Red Sox game. His mother, Robin, and I both braced for a young boy massacre of epic proportions. It never materialized.

When a person, especially a person on the left side of puberty, has a passion for some person, place or thing, it can be fabulously fierce.

Last week in Food Emporium I witnessed the meltdown of a tiny, blonde female toddler when she was not allowed to have a Scooby-Doo Pez dispenser, which hung directly at her eye level at the check-out counter. She was fondling it with longing as she simultaneously tugged on her daddy's shorts.

"Pez, pweeze! Pez pweeze!" she implored, saucer eyes gazing pleadingly upward.

"No, honey. Not today," answered her father, prying the Pez from her now vise-like grasp.

The accompanying scream was startling and anguished. Her red-faced dad pulled her away by the waist, her small arms outstretched achingly in Pez Scooby's direction as she cried "Nooooooooooo!," sounding like a lover wailing at her paramour's departure for war.

I recall the histrionics of me and my high school girlfriends when boyfriend disintegration would occur, as of course teenage relationships are wont to do. The physical and psychological pain seemed unbearable, and near animalistic-sounding sobbing felt like the only solution to rid the body of the toxins of rejection. As heartbreaking as it is for a 14-year-old girl, the rejection feels nearly as powerful for the powerless mother; the passion of the parent to protect is instinctive.

Often the attempt to protect a child from disappointment is futile. Losing, disenchantment and frustration are simply part and parcel of life. Without those three, joy would not seem as precious, and success not nearly as sweet.

Those pithy clichés—"Soldier on," "This too shall pass," "It could be worse," "Maybe next time,"—do little to rectify a passion purged at first blush. Yet I think the child will retain these time-worn and time-honored slogans each time they feel thwarted in the future. I want to believe that in their heart of hearts they know that they will live to see another day. That the odds of a team winning a championship again, or that a Pez Scooby-Doo will some day make it onto the check-out conveyer belt, are good.

The Yanks have made it to and won the World Series 20-something times before and the whole deal is a dream to be dreamed every year. I need to convince Jack to put a little more faith in the pinstriped boys of October.

Either that or move out until the playoffs are over. The latter sounds preferable.

Parenting on a "Grand" Scale

My husband phoned his mom this past Sunday to wish her happy Mother's Day. He put Jack and Janet on the line, and then it was my turn to share sweet motherly wishes. At one point she mused, "Well, I guess I'm the last grandmother they have." I quietly replied, "Yes," on my second motherless Mother's Day.

Grandparents are, well, *grand*. They're great. And lucky are the children who still have one or more alive and involved in their lives.

With both of my parents now gone, it is indeed Jon's parents who solely bear the mantle of grandparents. But my mother-in-law lives in Cyprus and my father-in-law in northern California; hardly over-the-river-and-through-the-woods. Jack and Janet see them perhaps once a year. The distance and the time difference haven't been ideally conducive to forming the close bond those children who live geographically closer to a grandparent experience.

Blake and Kenny were more fortunate. Their paternal grandparents lived less than an hour away. When they visited with their dad every-other-weekend they usually spent time with his parents, until their grandpa died when they were nine and 11. My parents lived locally for the first 10 and 12 years of the boys' lives, treating them to Broadway shows, New York City museums, helping them build school and Cub Scout projects, and taking them on countless ski trips. When my parents moved down to the northern neck of Virginia for what was to be the last two years of my dad's life, the boys spent a week with them each summer, reveling in the freedom of being away from us. They also loved the annual "Junk Food Day" that my parents allowed. After dad's death, and up until my mother's own death last year, she continued to sport the boys to adventurous trips abroad and otherwise, and stayed active in their lives.

I envy my younger children's friends whose grandparent(s) can visit often and vise-versa. It is so sweet to watch a grandpa coaching a third grade soccer team or notice a grandmother taking a granddaughter for a pedicure in town. Grandparents get to be parents again without having the ultimate responsibility, ergo; they get to be more fun. You know … great!

Janet's best friend Haley has both sets of grandparents living here in town. Her late father's parents, Judy and Tom, have been able to help Haley's full-time working mom with shuttling Haley around to various sports and social activities, as well as with getting her on and off the bus each day. They are present in her life, and I am sure Haley keeps them both feeling and looking young. I want to adopt them. Can a 50-year-old adopt two adorable 70-year-olds? I need to look into that.

I was fortunate enough to have my maternal grandmother around until I was 40 years old; my dad's father died when I was 32. My "Gramoo" thought I hung the moon and I felt the same about her. Even when she moved down to Florida, I would visit as frequently as possible. She and my father's father both invested in the magazine I founded, *County Kids,* and my Gramoo was all ears and a shoulder to cry on after my divorce in 1988.

I wish Janet and Jack could have had that grandparent familiarity, although I suppose my mom fit the bill for the better part of their 10 and 13-year-old lives.

Maybe Haley's grandparents could adopt them? Honorary grandkids? Well, maybe not, but it's still kind of a grand idea!

Doggone Predictable

Kids and pets: they're pretty much an inevitable combination. It could be a golden retriever or a gold fish, but at some point, your child is going to ask for a pet. Most likely you will buy one, and you may be fooled into believing that your kid will take on the lion's share of the caring and feeding for said pet. But really, mom (or dad)—the onus is all yours.

I am sure there are families who may strongly disagree with me, who will insist that their children bear the brunt of the pet responsibilities. Yet from my 22 years of experience, *I* have been the one who has cleaned up more pet poop, doled out more kibble, and cleaned up more crates, cages and fish bowls than I ever thought imaginable.

Kenny and Blake had rabbits, Beta fighting fish and a likable, but hyper dog, which we got from Adopt-a-Pet. The rabbits eventually died (not my fault; I was a good caretaker), ditto the fish. The dog, named Eli, seemed like a good idea. We bought her ostensibly for Blake's 10th birthday, and he was pretty consistent with feeding and the occasional dog-walk around the neighborhood. But it was I who would have to leave my office twice a day to check on her. She was so revved up from being alone that she wound up dragging me across the yard on my stomach; I was three months pregnant at the time. After being our family pet for about four months—many stomach rides, chewed up drapes, chair legs and shoes later—we arranged for her to be re-adopted by a wealthy family who spent weekends in the Hamptons; Eli made out well.

Janet pleaded for a puppy just before turning nine and so, four years ago, Glory, a black lab, came into our family. While Janet has for the most part lived up to her promise to love, honor and feed Glory, she refused to clean up after the puppy's accidents, which left that charming detail to yours truly. I can't blame her for not following through; it's gross. The training and the disciplining of Glory also fell on my shoulders, as does, of course, the majority of training and disciplining the children themselves.

This past Christmas, Jack was presented with a red fox lab that he named Joey. Here's the insane part—getting a new puppy was my idea. I am a martyr! Yes, Jack feeds Joey, plays with Joey and tries to help me with various behavior commands, but I am still president of the poop-and-pee patrol, the only member of our family that spends at least six to seven hours per day looking after Glory and Joey.

For all my griping here, caring for a pet is an important ritual for a child; it kind of prepares one for being a parent. Letting your kid choose a name, snuggle, play with, feed and help with any training of a pet gives a boost to their maturity, and in a way, their self-esteem. They are loved unconditionally and know that their pet is dependent upon them for love in return.

I have a close friend with a virtual menagerie of pets, from the furry to the feathered. Her twin boys are well-versed in respecting and caring for members of their family zoo, and this respect and caring has been ingrained into their personalities. Their mom—who, like me, works from home—is responsible during the school day for the assortment of pets, and one would think that she has had her fill of aviary-dwelling friends. But she too recently joined the puppy brigade!

Doggone it! Like kids, moms can still be a sucker for a furry little face.

Name Calling: When "CJ" is Really Christopher James

After my mother died and her obituary came out in the newspaper, Janet was surprised to learn by reading it, that Grandma Holly's real name was Nancy.

"Why did people call her 'Holly?'" she asked.

I explained that Holly was her middle name and Walker her maiden name. When she started a private high school back in the late 1940's, there was already a "Nancy Walker" at the school, so she chose Holly as her new first name.

"Sort of like me, right?" Janet queried. "How in preschool I went from 'Jessie' to 'Janet?'"

"Sort of, Jess," I replied to my daughter with the nickname I have called her since birth. And I recounted to her how that had worked.

When I was pregnant, my husband and I were doing the baby name search in several books, and we came upon the name "Jessie." We were both immediately taken by it. The definition intrigued and excited us all the more: *"Jessie. Dim. Jessica. Also, in Scotland, the diminutive of Janet."* Jon's maternal grandmother was a Scot named Janet (although her nickname was "Jenny"), and my business partner back in 1993 was named Janet. Perfect! We would name her Janet, honor both of these women, but call her Jessie. Are you confused?

Up until Janet was age five she was called Jessie by all. And then people began assuming her given name was Jessica. Although that is a lovely name, it was not my daughter's, and, at the time, it was a pretty popular name. So I made a knee-jerk reaction and asked her preschool teacher and her classmates to begin to call her Janet instead of Jessie. Jon and Jack began to call her by her given name as well, but Blake, Kenny and I were holdouts and continued to address her as Jess or Jessie. It may have been my idea to change to Janet but that didn't mean I could do it as easily as others. I still can't. I will not be surprised if Janet/Jessie has identity issues down the line.

If you are currently pregnant and mulling over names, my advice for you is to stick with whichever name it is you choose to call your child by and do not follow my experience. Name him Norman Joseph, but if you choose to address him as "NJ" then use that name forever (unless he's in trouble, of course, then it's the full mantle; my daughter knows when I sternly say, "Janet Holly Evans," she had better do as told). Realize too, that Christopher and Michael will most likely be shortened by a classmate or a teacher, just as Alison may become Ali, and Deborah can morph into Debbie.

Janet has a classmate known as Max, but his given name is Frank Maxwell, ergo, "Max." Once upon a time 40 years ago, there were lots of Franks and Janets and Bettys and Howards running about, but not so much anymore. So, his mom chose to call her baby boy Max and it really fits him and his personality. The same holds true for Janet's good friend, Eliza. Although her birth name is Eliza beth, she's really an Eliza kind of girl. And that's the key, even though when staring down at a one-minute-old infant face it can be difficult at best to make that name judgment call.

Luckily, with my youngest, Jack, we were able to make the call before he was even conceived. Although Janet/Jessie was only age two when that conception occurred, we already knew we should name the next child something we wouldn't have to explain. There was to be no Jonathan-Evans-but-we-call-him-Jack. He was to be just Jack, plain and simple.

Of course people can add a suffix to any moniker to create a nickname, so consider those as well. When Blake was in Marine Corps boot camp, a nasty drill instructor got right in his face and asked recruit Flannery his first name.

"Sir, Blake, sir!" shouted Blake expressionless.

"*Blake?*" the DI asked, a bit incredulously.

"Sir, yes, sir!"

"I bet your mom called you 'Blakey-Wakey' when you were a child, didn't she recruit?"

Blake says he grinned ever so slightly, in spite of himself. "Sir, yes, sir."

Yes, it seems Julie/Jul/Jules can turn even the most solid and serious of names into a playful, silly sing-song, proving that there is, indeed, plenty in a name.

Salute to Single Parents

Navigating the choppy waters of bringing up kids is hard enough with a co-captain. But riding the waves solo is a feat not for the faint of heart.

A parent may find themselves going it alone with children by choice, death of a spouse, or divorce (which, of course, is a choice as well). In the case of divorce or death, the initial experience is tinged with fear, sadness, trepidation and confusion. A friend who had a daughter out of wedlock some 20-odd years ago reports that those feelings were hers as well. Of course, there is always the ever-present joy that the child brings to the table, as well as the thread of hope, even if that hope seems dim and distant at first.

Nearly 21 years ago I found myself on the single parenting end of things. My first marriage was fraught with tension, disappointment and trauma, so after nearly five years of soldiering on, I moved out on my own with a two and four-year old in tow. It has always been that first morning that stays new and keeps it green for me.

Like most mornings with a very small child, I awoke to some low-grade whining and crying, as baby Kenny wanted his morning bottle of milk. Out of habit, I elbowed the space to my left. But instead of meeting up with a fleshy arm, a person who would get up to fetch the bottle because it was their turn to do the task, I felt only empty space. "Oh crap!" I murmured to myself, "I'm really on my own here."

Really on my own. Sure, there were many moments of "Yay!! I'm free!," yet these were always tempered by the demands and the logistics of having to seemingly be both parents at the same time, of working full-time in New York, and of juggling kids' schedules without the help of another adult. Until I hired a nanny. Even then though, I felt like an isolated figure.

When I see a single parent at school open houses, at a band concert, or on the sidelines at a child's athletic contest, I admire their bravery. In a Noah's Ark world of two-by-two they stand alone—sometimes literally—as other mothers and fathers hug or squeeze each other's hands when their offspring does something accomplished. As exhausting as it is for even the most married of us to be in a semi-single parent position when a spouse is off on a business or pleasure trip, it is most assuredly not the same. For our partner will be returning and the burden has a finite shelf life. For the single parent, the journey is almost always solitary, save for the every-other-weekend scenario of the divorced.

It's not always a "woe is me" situation and the single parent, above all, does not want sympathy (immediate sympathy following a spouse's unexpected or untimely demise is understood, of course). Empathy is fine. Empathy is like a mini support group meeting. But there is no woe in being able to have a child's undivided attention; there's no daddy or mommy with whom to "compete." Being a single parent, no matter what conditions put you in that category, is empowering. It is empowering to realize that you can get through the good, the bad and the ugly alone. It makes anything seem possible. You will discover that you can emerge out of the dark and into the light with grace and dignity intact or even, perhaps, newfound.

And sometimes—if you so choose—you emerge with a new partner to join you in parenting. Of course getting to *that* outcome is a task that most assuredly is not easy. Suffice it to say that my own journey from single to re-married parent was littered with uncomfortable laughter and a few more trips into heartbreak.

Along with the baggage that anybody brings into a relationship, there were two small parcels that no amount of camouflage could hide, nor did I want to hide them. They were/are as much a part of me as me. But to many men, those adorable little boys were deal breakers, and therein lay the heartbreak. Lucky for me, however, one brave and loving soul named Jon, took a deep breath and dove into instant parenthood.

There's a saying that "old age ain't for sissies," and neither is being a single parent. Rife with struggle, there are moments that are definitely darkest before the dawn, especially for the widowed. Yet no matter what the circumstance that leads to single parenting, you are— make no mistake about it—a force to be reckoned with. You carry a full load. And you trundle on even when the weight feels unbearable.

You are, simply, a singular sensation.

Reading: What a Concept!

In today's high-tech world, where kids under the age of about 16 can't remember *not* having a cell phone, a computer, a video game system, and cable TV with its choice of six cajillion stations, sitting down to read as entertainment or leisure has seemingly lost a lot of its luster and importance.

When I was a girl (jeez, how old do I sound?), reading was pretty much the only form of boredom busting. I loved reading the *Bobbsey Twins* and *Nancy Drew* series books, as well as Archie and Richie Rich comics. Another favorite series of mine was about a plucky young girl named Katie John, who briefly became my idol. I read to fall asleep, read on the beach, read when there was nothing interesting on the only four television stations offered back in the early to mid 1960's. Reading wasn't just a subject in school. Reading—especially for an aspiring writer-to-be—was as much a part of life as, well, breathing.

Not so much today. When I hear the inevitable "I'm bored" from my younger children my knee-jerk response is, "Go read a book!" Their usual response? "No! Are you kidding?! That's like school!" I then begrudgingly offer the litany of electronic pursuits, which they reject. This is followed by a disgusted and frustrated, "You are so spoiled. Go read!"

Reading isn't as second nature to my children as I would prefer. A couple of years ago I insisted that they each bring a book along on summer vacation and declared that at least one hour an evening be devoted to reading. I joined in with whatever book I happened to be enjoying. I also had them bring books to the beach and was delighted when they would tuck into them unprompted.

Blake and Kenny read a lot as younger kids; it wasn't the issue that it is in this new millennium. In third grade Blake began reading about the Civil War, graduating to books about World War 2, Navy Seals and the Vietnam War (good preparation for fighting in Iraq as a Marine). Kenny for a time was obsessed with the "Goosebumps" series, and it was as much about the reading as it was in collecting each book like so many baseball cards.

Jack the jock has been no surprise in being fond of books with a sports theme, whether a biography of Derek Jeter or Babe Ruth, or fiction about baseball, football or basketball. Last summer he broke from the expected and also devoured the Harry Potter series.

Janet was recently grounded, and without computer, phone, Ipod, friends over, and limited television, she began to read out of school in earnest. She found interest in the "Clique" and "Gossip Girls" tomes, reading one every other day. When she requested I go out and buy a new one, I happily obliged; it sure beat her asking for another lip-gloss or item of clothing. She has also begun pouring over *Pop Star* magazine and its ilk, as I had done decades before. Hey, reading is reading!

Children need to be reminded that television and the computer aren't the all and end all of stimulation and escape into another world. Books offer that and so much more. "Read" is the best four-letter word there can be.

The Dangerous World of Boys

If you've recently given birth to your first son, or if you're already a mom of say, an infant or toddler boy, this is a cautionary tale, a primer. It's a "buckle-your-seat-belts-you're-in-for-a-bumpy-ride" introduction to being a mother (or father) of the young male of the species.

Boys and bumps, bruises, breaks and bloody cuts seem—in my experience—to go hand-in-hand.

Out of my three sons, so far my son Kenny takes the prize in the becoming wounded department. When Kenny was age one, Blake chucked a Matchbox car at him resulting in a butterfly stitch to the forehead. At age four, Kenny broke his tibia and mind-blowingly repeated that break a scant two years later. At seven, Blake accidentally (yeah, right) slammed Kenny's fingers in a door, resulting in yet another break and half a dozen stitches. At 11, he broke his arm falling off a swing. When he was 15, he sprained that same arm, and at age 19, badly cut one hand after a freak fall on his way back to his apartment after class.

Clearly some boys are more accident prone than others. Blake survived childhood with only a few stitches and bumps, and—considering he has been in combat three times since 2003—has emerged with only the most minor of injuries. But the first time your child, your son, gets a bad boo-boo it's almost as painful for you. The first sign of a break or of blood gives new meaning to the term "adrenaline rush."

If your son is an athlete, well, try and prepare yourself for the inevitable injury, although admittedly, I'm not entirely sure how one prepares oneself. The least of it may be a bad bruise. But there, lurking in the air on the field of play, may be the breakage of a limb, an errant ball flying into your son's nether regions, a bloody nose or blackened eye; momentary unconsciousness. Now these are the worst cases and should not in any way, shape or form mean you prohibit sports from your child's agenda. Because—trust me—even the most seemingly ordinary of moments at home may cause temporarily traumatic injury.

Case in point: On this past Sunday, as I was folding laundry and my husband, Jon, was paying bills, a blood-curdling scream emanated from our garage. Janet began yelling for us: "Mom! Dad! Jack's hurt! Jack's hurt!" As I ran into the garage, there was Jack holding his left hand, blood spewing from one of his fingers. "I closed it in the door! Omigod! Help!" As he was going out the side door of our garage, he had accidentally slammed the door shut on his fingers, specifically, the middle finger (pretty appropriate for how he felt at that moment). We bundled his hand in a towel and ice, and Jon dashed him to the hospital. By the grace of God, I decided to immediately begin cleaning up all the blood in the garage. As I did, I looked down and there staring up at me was the top quarter of Jack's finger! We had no idea that it had been severed. The bottom line is that most of it was stitched back on and I'm sure he'll be playing baseball in no time. But, wow—dashing part of my kid's finger to the hospital resulted in a billion new grey hairs and a heart that nearly popped right out of me and my car and onto the highway.

Ah, boys. Here's what you need to do as soon as you birth one: Stock your medicine cabinet with bandages, gauze, Neosporin, hydrogen peroxide, a finger splint, an ace bandage, several ice packs and arnica. Stock your liquor cabinet with whiskey or wine, or load up your freezer with pints of your favorite ice cream (pick your poison) for you to ingest after the accident. Keep in mind that you should probably breathe while the initial ouchiness ensues. Don't let your boy catch you crying, and keep reminding yourself that things will be okay. This too shall pass.

A Death in the Family

I was 12 years old when I first experienced a death in my immediate family. My grandfather died of cancer. My memories of that event are of sadness and confusion as I stood in our kitchen while my mother wept, and my father did all the talking. And then they were suddenly gone for a week, and I never understood why my brother and I couldn't also go to say "goodbye."

Two weeks ago my mother died. My children knew that she was going to die, that she had an incurable disease; ALS. The grandfather Janet and Jack were too young to remember had also died of ALS eight years earlier and they had heard the stories of what this hideous and insidious disease had done to Grandpa Butler. Oddly enough, we learned of mom's diagnosis on the same day we learned our 13-year-old dog was also soon to die.

It is at once difficult and easy to explain death to a child. The concept of death is terrifying to both young and old and yet it is inevitable. My three-year-old niece, Faith, seemed to understand that Grandma Holly was no longer going to visit with her and sing. She released a balloon the day after Holly died exclaiming, "Gramma is with Gawd. She is in Heaben!" Janet, however, also age three when my father died, was unsure about what had happened then. Instead of bringing her down to Virginia—where my father had died and where his cremains were scattered—we opted to leave her at home with a sitter and her then-baby brother Jack. She, like me decades before, was never to say a full "goodbye."

My sons Blake and Kenny were ages 13 and 11 when my father was diagnosed with ALS. At first I felt I should protect them from the truth and I simply explained that Grandpa was very sick, it made me very sad, and that was why I was crying a lot. About two weeks after the diagnosis, when my former husband brought them home from a weekend visitation, he pulled me aside and said, "Look, the kids know something is up ... Kenny heard you on the phone talking about your dad dying. You should tell them the truth. Don't sugar coat it." He was right, and so the truth I told. It made what was to come much easier.

What is to come and what is right there at the end of a life that is trapped in a failing body is almost too surreal to put into words. My mother kept repeating to me and my brother that "the roles are reversed." And, indeed, we were helping her to walk, interpreting what she was trying to say, spooning ice chips into her mouth, and getting her dressed.

One morning, a week before she died, I picked out an outfit for her that was all pink. I knew she might not be thrilled. All she was able to do was crinkle up her nose in distaste at my selection. I joked that it was payback for all the times she dressed me up in horribly stiff petticoats underneath impossibly frilly dresses. She laughed, and then wore the pink without further complaint.

As my mom faded, I was away from home and my children for the better part of two weeks. Roles were reversed there too, as Jon got to experience my job. But I did speak with the kids every night, filling them in on Grandma's decline and my sadness, and when the end finally came, there were tears heard over the telephone and big hugs upon my return.

I was unable to be with my father when he died. He left this world at exactly the moment I pulled out of my driveway on the trip down to see him. But I was able to fully be there with and for my mother as she took her last breath and she and my father reunited. Her death—as many deaths do—has taught me about life and about how I want to relate to my own children.

My mom died on my birthday. It is a horrifying thought at first and yet it was a final parental gift. Just before her last breath I was alone with her in a hospital room, just as we had been some 40-something years before. Mother and child about to embark on a magical journey, only this time, it would be one without the other.

When Agendas Collide

It begins almost imperceptibly. You want to zig when your child wants to zag. "Too bad," you implore. "I'm the adult and you're the child. We're going to do what I want." Fireworks, detonation, whatever you want to call it, ensue. And after several cataclysmic scenes such as this, it begins to dawn on you—or at least it should—that your kid is growing up and probably has a right to their own agenda once in a while.

Testing the waters, performing and perfecting their baby steps into breaking away as a 'tween and young teen, is natural. Although as a parent we may not completely want to encourage the freedom ("I'm losing my baby!"), we really have to do just that, and we need to grow as well.

On a family vacation, we may have the plan to visit this monument and that site; eat at that restaurant Joe in accounting recommended; ski from dawn to dusk; rent canoes and paddle miles downstream until we reach that place our neighbor said was "spectacular." The kids, however, have something that may be altogether different in mind: hit a historic site or two and then just wander down whatever street looks interesting; grab a falafel from a brightly colored cart; stop skiing early to chill back in the room, or in a hot-tub. And think about it—it's their vacation, too. Why shouldn't they be allowed their opinion and a certain amount of unstructured time?

I recall going on a short cruise to the Bahamas at age 16 with my parents and my brother, then age 14. My brother wanted to sneak into the casinos and I wanted desperately not to be on vacation with my "embarrassing" parents and my "stupid" little brother. My parents, to their credit, gave us a little rope—I could sunbathe alone and not next to my pasty-white folks, my brother wandered about the ship from stem to stern, successfully getting in some illegal slot-machine time. I flirted with the junior waiter, much to my dad's chagrin, but he then allowed me to take a motor-scooter ride with the cockney-speaking lad in Nassau! What a great vacation after all!

As our children morph into middle schoolers and then high schoolers, we need to check and maybe re-check our motives for wanting certain sports or activities in which our offspring be engaged. When Kenny was a fifth grader and eligible to perform in middle school musicals I wanted him to follow in the thespian footsteps of his Butler grandparents and, luckily, he took to the stage like a duck to water. Janet, however, balked at trying out for the musical last year, but this year will be "Singing in the Rain" with the rest of her buddies. I encouraged her trying out be sure, and then I let her close friends do the final persuading. Blake loved playing basketball, but after his junior year in high school decided to opt out. I couldn't imagine such a thing, and pleaded with him to go for it again. Was he a star? No. Was he enjoying it anymore? No. But I loved sitting in the bleachers at my alma mater, pretending to be a 16-year-old cheerleader again, watching teenage boys dribble and shoot. How could he deny me that? Yet he did, and it was all for the best; it made me decide to finally "graduate" and move to on.

When parent and child agendas—both literal and metaphorical—collide, it can be ugly and awkward and just plain unpleasant. One or both sides will usually spit out the phrase, "You are *so* selfish!" And then each should really go to their respective corners and take a breath. Like Rocky Balboa, it's probably better to end the fight in a split decision, rather than a knockout.

Give it your best shot, but end with a full heart.

Teaching My Jock to be a Good Sport

My eight-year-old son, Jack, is a jock-of-all-trades. I don't think he's met a sport he didn't love. Since he was four or five he has watched ESPN in the mornings and afternoons instead of cartoons. His room is decorated pillowcase to light switch with sports balls. Of all my children, Jack appears to be the most natural athlete and he puts incredible intensity into all of the sports he tries. His passionate competitive streak, however, needs some taming.

If Jack's beloved Yankees lose, he screams and yells and throws things about the family room. "Ahrrg! Yankees!," he cries at the television. "I can't believe they lost!" His crying is so mournful and deep that my husband and I have to turn away with stifled laughter. I always hear him whining at his sports-oriented video games when the electronic device beats him. And when he first lost a soccer game in kindergarten, he claimed that they had actually tied, not lost. There was no convincing him otherwise. Luckily for him—and I suppose for us—his first grade soccer team won all their games. His basketball team didn't keep score in first grade. Then along came second grade and the score counted in both sports.

We counseled Jack that his fall soccer team may not have the same championship season as the year prior. "If you lose, you cannot detonate in front of the other players." We told him it was perfectly okay not to win. That comment was greeted with quite the scowl.

Jack's coach last fall was a gracious, lovely older gentleman. He stressed the importance of having fun in addition to playing hard. It was pretty refreshing. Sure, for our family's sake, I wish they had won more than one game all season, yet the absence of the "win-win-win at all costs" attitude was a welcome respite. My husband, Jon, and I braced ourselves after that first loss, waiting for Jack to meltdown in the company of his peers and our friends. But it didn't happen. Sure, he pouted and stomped back at home, but on the field he seemed oddly (for him) okay with not winning. He had still played at full tilt and continued to do so game after losing game after losing game. When basketball season started—and the team both won some and lost some—he was publicly a good sport on the losing days.

"Wow," I thought," this is progress!"

Of course as I write this he is screaming at his father while he plays a baseball X-Box game. "Cheater! Dad you're a cheater!" he is bellowing. "It's not fair!" Jeez, how am supposed to write with all that racket? But we have ceased to coddle him and let him win. His brothers, sisters, uncles all used to lose on purpose because the scene that erupted once Jack lost was so excruciating. But he—and all boys and girls—need to learn that winning *isn't* everything. Winning isn't the *only* thing. Winning is just *one* of the things.

I know that I have learned more from losing in the sports arena as well as in the arena of life. Sure, it's more fun to win, but the reality is that for there to be a winner, there also has to be a loser. That's just the fact. I know that Jack will absorb that concept eventually. For now I have to be happy that his implosions do not occur on the field or on the court.

Just yesterday, after his soccer team won, he said, "Max was being a bad sport. He started pushing everybody when he lost." "You wouldn't do that, right?" I asked. "No," he replied with a tinge of annoyance. "It's just a *game*, mom!" Exactly.

Roots, Wings and Other Things

The phrase, "there are two things we must give our children, roots and wings," has been dancing around in my head lately. As I hit the streets and the internet in search of the perfect holiday gifts for my four kids, I ponder if I have given enough roots and wings; something money can't buy and Santa can't deliver.

Sometimes guilt overwhelms me when I think about my older two, Blake and Kenny. I divorced their father when they were just ages two and nearly four. For five years I struggled and survived as a single parent; we were fairly rootless for a while. But when I remarried 12 years ago, my husband Jon and I were able to start providing them with family traditions. As a real hands-on stepfather, Jon instilled in them a sense of responsibility as well as a living illustration of setting and attaining goals. I, in turn, was able to involve them in the creative process associated with my then-business (*County Kids* magazine) and of the joy and hard work involved in seeing a dream through to fruition.

The actual physical roots my children had were first planted in my hometown of Weston, Connecticut; we also lived in the same house in which I had grown. But five years ago, knowing instinctively that it was time for me to "graduate" from Weston, we pulled up roots and settled here in New Canaan. Now firmly planted they—and we—are thriving in our new environment. Blake and Kenny will always have a pull towards Weston, as will I, and it is another bond the three of us share.

Giving our children wings is a more emotionally difficult task than roots. Do we push them out of the nest or nudge them gently? I believe each child is unique, and the method for teaching them about freedom can vary. Partly, we teach by example, by flying solo with determination, or by breaking away with hesitation, i.e. not taking many trips without them. Neither way is the better way, but each way helps them develop the wings they will need. Wings that invariably appear to flap when we are least prepared.

When Blake began talking about a career in the military during his sophomore year in high school, the flutters caught me unawares. And on that morning in July of 2001, when the doorbell rang at 4 a.m. and his Marine recruiter arrived to drive him to boot camp, my heart couldn't have been fuller or more broken. Blake was ready to soar and I let go, but not without holding on to a couple more feathers.

Although Janet and Jack are still here, continuing to grow their roots and wings, I miss my older birds and have been adjusting slowly, but surely, to my half-empty nest.

Traditions and family in-jokes during the holidays remind our family of its roots. But the moment I cherish most in this world—where roots and wings come together for this mommy—is on Christmas morning.

It has been a tradition for many years now, that on December 25th, whichever child wakes up first must come to our room and tell us that he/she thinks or knows (by peeking) that Santa has come. That child then gently wakes up the other three and then all four of them pile into our bed for at least another half an hour of sleep. Christmas of 2002 is the last time all four children were home, as Blake was in Japan last year. That morning is etched in my mind and in my heart. There we were, from then three foot tall Jack to six footer Blake, all snuggled together in the silent still of the morning, anticipatory, sleepy, giggling, and lovingly making fun of one another; my winged and my still wingless birds safe in my embrace if for but a temporary slice of time.

I envision this tradition continuing in years to come, with grandchildren and daughters and sons-in-law, all piled onto our bed in the wee hours of Christmas morn. Roots going back deeply and feathers floating lightly above the bed. It is my favorite Christmas gift. It is simple and it is priceless.

It is truly, the root of my happiness.

Birth Order Myths and Maybe-Truths

Since the days of Cain and Abel, birth order has fascinated us and formed who we are, perhaps what career we choose, as well as our relationships with siblings, our spouse, and with our friends. Along with the genes and personality traits that our parents pass along, the order in which they conceived and popped us out into this world helps to make us who we are.

There are variables, however, to the theory that the firstborn are usually more responsible, smarter and strive to please more than second-or-third born. Or that middle children have less of a clear-cut role in the family, or even that the youngest expects others to make decisions for him, therefore takes on less responsibility. Often the sex of the child, as well as the dynamics in blended, single or divorced families, throws a wrench into the accepted birth order suppositions.

My own four children are a bit all over the map in terms of birth order traits. Blake, the firstborn, enlisted in the Marines right out of high school, so clearly he took on a leadership role in life, as well as in the family. He was always the peace keeper and protector growing up and remains as such. One website I visited on birth order states that the firstborn may respond to the birth of the second child by feeling unloved and neglected. Blake reacted to Kenny's birth by chucking a Matchbox car at the baby's face, resulting in a butterfly stitch to the forehead. There were other such incidents until each reached their teens; they are now the best of friends.

Kenny has the distinction of having been the youngest for eight years until I remarried and had his sister, Janet. Her birth catapulted him to the position of the middle child, a rank that's often described as "discouraged, becoming the 'problem child.'" Acting out for the middle kid is described as a way to garner back his or her parents' attention. Spot on for Kenny. And Janet—who not only shares Kenny's status as middle child, but also shares his birth date—has revealed some of those tendencies as well, though not as strongly as her brother.

Janet, like Kenny, had/has a double place in the hierarchy of my children in that she is the oldest of the Evans' kids, so she shares many firstborn traits, too, which can counteract the characteristics of the typical middle child. Being the only girl throws in a whole different set of actions (and hormonal reactions) to the sibling mix. Her older brothers at first protected and coddled her, then felt she was a royal pain, and now for the most part have reverted back to their original nurturing ways. How we, her parents, deal with her also has a direct correlation to her birth order(s), sex, and of additionally being a part of a family with two older half-siblings.

"Baby" Jack really doesn't exhibit the typical traits of the youngest in the family, but he has experienced the inevitable parental responses to being the last child born. While Blake's baby book is filled to the brim with duly noted milestones and dozens of photos, I couldn't even begin to tell you where Jack's is located in the attic (or is it the basement?). It merely notes his size and weight, and includes those inked newborn feet the hospital produces. I can recite the time of birth, birth weight and length of Blake, Kenny and Janet, but draw a blank on Jack's vital newborn statistics. I don't recall his first word and almost always forget to bring my camera to school events or to the field of play! His sibling's landmarks are memorialized and memorized properly.

The birth order experts postulate that the baby of the family usually feels smallest and weakest, unable to take on responsibilities, but nothing could be farther than the truth for my youngest guy. In fact, one birth order site reveals that: "Unburdened by the high expectations that many parents have for their eldest children, many youngest experience greater successes than their siblings, or they will make their mark in life in a very individualistic way." That's my baby!

A competitive will, a free spirit, a sense of superiority, a need to be babied—all of these things can, and often are, explained by birth order. So many forces collide to shape our personalities, our approach to life, and it's spellbinding to watch it all in the faces of our children.

"Location, location, location." It's not just a real estate mantra, is it?

3
SCHOOL DAYS

Making Memories on the School Bus

One of my most precious memories of the first day of school was seeing the big, yellow bus slowly wind its way around the corner of the street on which I lived. It was as if at the very moment I climbed up the bus steps, I was "at school." My friends would be saving me a seat and we had a small chunk of time on the bus to access the physical changes that had occurred over the summer in other people and, of course, in ourselves.

I still get a tiny thrill as I have waited at the bus stop over the past 17 years with one or more of my children. Even when the kids eventually banned me from waiting with them, I still snuck a peek out the front door, waiting to hear that familiar squeaking of the bus breaks as it neared our driveway. Of all the things my tax dollars pay for, the school bus is one of the best: convenience for me and socialization for my kids all in one.

But late last fall, and into the past winter, I suddenly and insidiously found myself driving Janet to middle school every morning, leaving the poor school bus to pause at our driveway and then carry on Janet-less. It began when she missed the bus one morning. She quite enjoyed the chauffeured ride, and I started using the lure of the mommy-drive when mysterious ailments threatened to keep her from going to school. I got sucked in and it, well, sucked!

When we moved a few miles down the road in the early spring I finally came back to my parental senses and told her that the bus was the only option for getting to school. After a couple of initial fits and starts, she once again began the wait for the bus, and her hopping back on gave me all manner of a sense of freedom.

I loved riding the school bus in elementary school, even though my trepidation as a kindergartner first threatened that enjoyment. But my wonderful first bus driver, Mr. Peachtree (seriously his name!), allowed me for a time to sit next to him up front, inches from the steering wheel. There was some kind of small steel bench next to the driver's seat, and on my very first day riding the bus, he helped me up the steps, picked me up and plunked me down on that bench. I felt special and safe—although Lord knows by today's standards riding up there would be everything but safe!

Riding the school bus allowed my friends and I precious time to unwind after school; learn to be tolerant of the occasional bully; exchange confidences, hear the latest joke. As I got older and into high school, I could doze for a few minutes in the morning and hold my boyfriend's hand in the back of the bus on the way home. Admittedly, once I turned 16 and could then drive my own vehicle to school, I happily gave up my seat on the bus, yet it had served me and my parents very well for 11 years. And I still, to this day, miss old, kind Mr. Peachtree.

We now live a mere two minute drive from the elementary school where Jack will be a fourth grader, but the bus is how he will get to school and back, even if it takes 15 or 20 minutes for it to complete its route. It's time for Jack to socialize with old and new friends alike and, as a fourth grader, finally get to sit in the back seat and make faces at those who choose to drive their kids to school.

This school year, I am looking forward to the extra half-hour to 45-minutes I will gain by letting the yellow bus transport Janet and Jack. They will be making memories while I will be making better use of my time. It seems a win-win.

An Ode to Male Elementary School Teachers

This is a "love note" of a sort to those few, those proud, those male elementary school teachers. My youngest child, Jack, now a third grader, has had the good fortune of having two male teachers in a row. I say "good fortune" not to be disrespectful of all the very capable and special female teachers he has had and will have in the future. But "good fortune" because both Mr. Patrick Murren and Mr. Darren Bruce have helped to turn him around, bringing him out of his shell and increasing his confidence in learning. This is not to say a woman couldn't have done the same thing, yet the male-on-male dynamic just happened to have worked well with my son.

I was in the fourth grade when I was assigned my first male teacher. Ronald Caruso was then the only male teacher in the whole elementary school. At first, I was nervous; a male teacher was such a rarity—what if he was really mean or stricter than the women? But Ron Caruso had something going for him that held this then nine-year-old girl spell-bound, for Mr. Caruso was young, dark and handsome. All of the girls in the class were smitten, so much so, that at the end of the year, several of us pitched in and purchased him a signet ring!

Mr. Caruso had more than just a pretty face, however. He had an equally attractive way of engaging all of us in his class. The teacher I had in third grade used a more fear-based way of teaching; Mr. Caruso was more respect-based. He didn't threaten, yet he was nevertheless no nonsense. He knew I could do better, and he encouraged me with my strengths (writing) and was patient with me with my weaknesses (math and science). Learning became fun, not just mandatory. And his respect-based manner made it easier for me down the line when I encountered different teaching styles in middle and high school. Mr. Caruso also played with us at recess, another rarity among teachers. He even presided over a mock wedding of me and fourth grade boyfriend at recess!

For Jack, my little jock, throwing a football with Mr. Murren at recess was a highlight of second grade. Any adult who spends time with Jack on a sport is his hero, but the act of tossing the ball with him humanized Mr. Murren for Jack. He was a teacher to be respected, but he was also a fun guy. Hearing about it from Jack made me smile to know his teacher had connected with him.

All last summer Jack spoke incessantly about Mr. Bruce. "I hope I get him, mom," he would say almost daily. And when the letter from the school arrived with his teacher assignment, he beamed. Lately, however, he has been having mysterious head and stomach aches—imagined, not at all real. Just before the holiday vacation he pulled the headache card, but I drove him to school anyway. After several public scenes, I was able to get him to his locker. Magically, Mr. Bruce appeared out of the classroom and gently got Jack to take off his coat to begin the day, as I gratefully retreated down the hall.

Now, I know that a female could have had the same effect on Jack's behavior, but as I have said, there is just something I can't articulate about a male teacher's effect on my son or on myself, for that matter. It's not better—it's just fundamentally different. Just like with a female teacher, sometimes the chemistry between teacher and student works, and sometimes it is woefully non-existent. With the latter, all one can do as a parent and a student/child is hope for the best given the circumstances; make lemonade out of a lemon.

The salaries for all teachers, male *or* female, are disturbingly low given that their profession, their job—teaching our children—is one of the more important tasks in life. And, as reverse sexist as this is going to sound, (and I apologize in advance), for a man to choose to be an educator at any level, let alone the elementary school level, is a choice to be applauded. Supporting a family, let alone oneself, on a teacher's salary is no easy feat. But teaching is a passionate profession. The male teachers I have thus far encountered have made that evident. And their passion for teaching has thus far developed a passion for learning in Jack. For that, I will be forever thankful.

The Over Scheduled Child

School starts soon and with it, all of those after school activities. Classes and sports of which your child may or may not have asked to participate. Activities that may leave little or no down time at home after the school day is done.

There's football or soccer; field hockey or karate; drama classes, voice or piano lessons, gymnastics, cheerleading or acting. There's science enrichment, a foreign language program, or an art experience. Most likely your child is enrolled, registered, and otherwise involved in more than one of the above.

Not that there's anything wrong with that. I've got four kids; I know what it's like. You want them busy—idle hands are the devil's tool—and you want them to have a taste of, and hopefully an aptitude for, sports and/or the arts or to encourage academic fortification.

Sometimes, though, it's too much. And occasionally it's our agenda and not theirs that's really at play.

When I was a kid, there weren't very many options for after school activities other than riding bikes, playing in the woods or just hanging with friends at my house or theirs. I had Girl Scouts once a week and ballet on Saturdays. A couple of my buddies had piano or other musical instrument lessons. No recreation department sports existed, only pick-up football or baseball games on the very few playing fields. It wasn't until high school that more sports were available for the offing when the final class bell rang, as well as yearbook or literary magazine or Latin clubs.

As soon as my first two children reached elementary school, I couldn't wait for them to partake of the smorgasbord of goings on in the afternoon hours. They had karate, soccer, art classes, and Cub Scouts. I foolishly thought it would buy me more time at work when school ended, but instead I found myself driving hither and thither like a headless chicken. I'd sometimes dash back to my office to call a client or put out a fire, and then peal out again to pick up and re-deliver a boy to the next field or building.

As is usually the case for a parent with multiple children, I learned my lesson from the first two, and eased up a bit on Janet and Jack's extracurricular activities. Still, we made Janet play soccer for a few fall seasons even though she clearly didn't enjoy it, and I kept Jack enrolled in karate long after its appeal had waned.

At the beginning of the current school year's launch, Janet made it clear that she wanted more time at home after school and chose only two activities, with only one falling during the week. Mostly she wanted and needed to unwind from seven-plus hours of school work. I need to respect and honor that, even though I'd prefer that she indulge in some of the things I wish I'd had offered to me at her age. But, with just Jack to shuttle about to and from sports, I actually find that I have that extra time for work and other mundane, yet necessary responsibilities.

Over scheduling the kids equals over scheduling the mom. Every child needs to regroup for a while once they hop off the bus. Tucking into a juice box and a snack for half an hour only to "hurry-up-and-get-ready" for (fill in the blank) more than two or three times a week gets tiresome, literally.

The detonation of your child isn't worth the price of admission to physical or cultural or academic enrichment. Take what you (or they) can, and leave the rest.

Surviving "Snow Days"

I look forward with such unmitigated glee to the end of the holiday vacation. That first week of January promises that children will be back in school and I will have at least six hours of "Julie-time." But, inevitably, that euphoria is cut excruciatingly short thanks to another mother—Mother Nature. The snow begins to dribble or dump and suddenly the kids are home early, go in later, or are home for the entire day altogether.

I'm not such an old fuddy-duddy that I don't remember the thrill of a "snow day" as a child. Except back then we didn't have nearly as many days off as my children have had during their school career. My friends and I waited for the bus in bundles of clothes and winter boots while the snow flew around us. There were plenty of mornings when we would watch the flakes swirl thick outside our classroom window, but the school day was never cut short. I have to admit it was sort of exciting to be on the bus during snowstorms, going slowly down the windy roads, the chains on the bus tires jingling like bells on Santa's sleigh. But, that was then and this is now.

Now means even the report of a possible snowstorm can cause school to be cancelled. During the winter the kids watch the weather channel as if the best cartoon in the universe were on. Even if it snows on a Saturday, they are convinced that school won't be in session come Monday morning.

I practically break out in a sweat on snow-draped mornings watching the local television station's school closing scroll across the bottom of the TV screen. Our town's name starts with an "N," so as soon as the schools beginning with "M's" start appearing, my heartbeat quickens, and I hold my breath and cross my fingers. If New Canaan is indeed cancelled I let out a guttural cry and flop back onto the bed. There go all my plans and appointments for the day.

So, how to survive a snow day? I actually don't have any concrete advice. Survival all depends upon the ages of your children. When any and all of mine were of nursery school and younger elementary school age, making it through the day without losing my mind and my hair meant bundling all of us up and playing out in the snowy yard for a while. This would be followed up with hot soup, hot chocolate, board games and a couple hours of Nickelodeon. As they have gotten older—and if the driving conditions permit—we will take in a matinee, or, failing that, rent a movie or two. I know it's not ideal to depend upon the television as a babysitter, but it nevertheless allows me to get some writing done, return phone calls and perform household chores uninterrupted. And, always, dividing and conquering means less conflicts between siblings, so I will arrange to swap one of my kids for a friend's kid. Everybody's happy.

Well, not exactly everybody. I am happier and more productive when the kids are in school Monday through Friday. January seems unusually full of school delays, early dismissals and out and out no school. And then, before you know it, February break rolls around!

Winter should be a time to appreciate snow: Tranquility! Skiing! Cozy fires! But for this mom it more often than not causes cringing and crankiness, not my more attractive traits to be sure. Lucky for me, the kids find the cringe and the crank hilarious. Perhaps that's their way of surviving *me!*

Teenager on Board

My nest is now three-quarters empty.

Last weekend we drove our daughter, my third child Janet, up to a boarding school in Massachusetts to begin the second semester of her freshman year in high school. A new chapter begins for both her and the rest of the family, at least the three of us left at home: me, her dad and younger brother, Jack.

My husband attended boarding school during his high school years, but I was a public high school kid. Where Janet was concerned, we had batted the idea of a boarding school back and forth over the past year, with Jon being more pro and me more or less on the fence. I knew it would probably be best for her academically. But I kind of enjoyed the public high school social experience and, for better or worse, also liked having her around. Plus, I found pleasure in seeing her buddies both here at our house as well as out and about in town. I miss them already.

The decision to withdraw her from the high school and enroll in boarding school happened quickly. She asked if she could go, our batting around ceased, and the search for the right school increased. And within two weeks it was done. Boom! Instant teen on board.

It's a big decision, this one of sending your child off to a private, residential secondary school. All sorts of factors—financial, academic, emotional, and social—must be considered. Often the decision isn't so monumental. Many families come from a long line of boarding school graduates, from great grandparents down to the current generation, so the conclusion of where to spend the high school years is foregone. Jon's family had that kind of history. Mine is mixed—mom attended boarding school in New Orleans, and my dad graduated from a public high school; my brother had a boarding education as a middle schooler. And, as I said, I am a happy grad of a local high school here.

Often a student needs a smaller, more concentrated classroom environment in which to succeed, and private or residential schools can accomplish this more readily than a public school. A stricter dress code and/or discipline expectations may also be easier to enforce in a private school setting than at home or in the local middle or high school. Oftentimes, boarding school traditions are embraced by the parent who has been down that road and they would like those customs visited on their children.

We have friends in town—in fact the mom is a former classmate of Jon's from The Kent School—who have sent both of their children to their mother's alma mater. Although they miss the kids, the concept of them going away to school was hardly foreign. Dad got teary at the prospect of an empty home initially, but I think now he's adjusted. I may need some advice from him on how to do just that.

Our second oldest son also went away during his junior year, only to return to and graduate from the high school, so this is not my maiden voyage with the whole kid-away-at-boarding-school. But somehow it feels different. And raw.

While there are certain things I will not miss—arguments over computer curfew time, or appropriate school attire, and being tense every morning, wondering whether or not she would make the school bus—I will miss her, the Janet-ness of her, on a daily basis. Things such as the unexpected hugs and giggles just for me; the sharing of friend "drama;" the scoop on the Jonas Brothers; the hormones that coincide with my own; the fact that my eye liner, or favorite pair of Uggs, or body scrub will not be disappearing.

As we said goodbye to her last Sunday in front of her dorm, I was paradoxically both of full heart and heart-*broken*. I hugged her maybe a second longer than I think she was comfortable with and as I pulled away tears immediately filled my eyes. Janet winced.

"It's okay, mom," she said, turning a little pink nonetheless. I thought of the lyrics to her favorite Billy Ray Cyrus/Miley Cyrus song ("Ready, Set, Don't Go"):

(MILEY): Lemme go now. (BILLY RAY): Don't go! (MILEY): I'll be alright, I'll be ok. Know that I'll be thinkin' of you each and every day. (BILLY RAY): She's gotta do what she's gotta do ... (MILEY): This is where you don't say what you want so bad to say ... (BILLY RAY): This is where I want to but I won't get in the way. Of her and her dream. And spreadin' her wings ...
(MILEY): I'm ready to fly!

I will learn to get more on board with the child away at school. Change is good. And if nothing changes, nothing changes.

4
TECHNOLOGY TALES

Cell-ing Out? Kids and Telephones

On the Christmas that I turned 12, the big present from my parents was a baby blue princess-style telephone and my own separate number. It was thrilling, it was slightly outrageous, and it was a rarity among my friends; only one other classmate had her own phone and separate number. The year was 1968. Oh, we were so hip!

Flash forward some 35 years and my soon-to-be 12-year-old daughter is asking, pining, campaigning, and bargaining for her own telephone. But not one in the house, mind you; she got that this summer when we plugged her own version of a princess phone into our rarely-used fax line. No, she wants her own cellular telephone. Because "everybody has one."

"Well, if everybody has one," I have replied repeatedly, "You can borrow theirs to call me from town." This results in a huge roll of the 11-year-old eyes, a whip of the hair and heavy stomping out of the room. Even my eight-year-old, Jack, says that he is saving his money to buy a cell phone.

Am I really losing it? Is my common sense out-of-date? Why would a child—who doesn't drive, doesn't hold a job to pay for the monthly fee, and who is never anywhere that I haven't already dropped him or her off—need a cell phone?

Maybe I am stuck in the 20th century. I could be; this century is a mere four years young. Perhaps I am being as un-hip as those peers of my parents who thought their buying me my own telephone line in seventh grade was way over-the-top. "You're so spoiled," kids would say to me. I preferred to look at it as being lucky. And my parents looked at it as a way to own their home telephone again (I was quite the chatty kid).

When Kenny turned 15, we broke down and got him and Blake their own phone line, and, at 16—on the brink of driving and working very part-time—Kenny got a cell phone. During his senior year, the cell came in handy for me to track him down on weekend evenings. Blake, much to my frustration, has never been keen on wanting a cell phone or even a land-line in his Marine barracks. It was one thing not to call when he was in combat in Iraq, but now that he's back in the U.S. of A., a phone call more than once a month would be helpful. I think if any child of mine is getting a cellular telephone for Christmas this year, it will be him. Ah, but I digress.

I have queried Janet regarding the merits of having her own cell phone and she typed up a full page of her perceived benefits: "I have about the amount of money for this specific piece of responsibility and I will keep saving up to pay for the service … I am old enough for one because everyone my age has one." (I know that this statement is a gross exaggeration, having spoken to close to a dozen of her sixth grade classmate's parents). She concluded that it would be helpful because when she is walking into town, or is at a friend's house, she could communicate with me.

Help me, fellow parents. In my mind, her having a cell phone seems so unnecessary. If I worked out of the home full-time and she was a latch-key kid, perhaps I would see the need. But there are land lines at her friend's houses, and if friends have a cell, then she can use theirs to call me, or just go plunk a couple quarters into a pay phone, or even borrow a merchant's telephone! I feel both on the fence and yet securely on the side of "no." Do I sell (cell) out?

It's a different age our children live in now. The year 1968 and its sensibilities seems so very far away, and of course in fact they are. But I still have trouble reconciling with my young daughter's view of a cellular phone as the ultimate accessory.

E.T.: Phone home with an answer for me!

OMG! Mom's a Technophobe!

"Technophobe: fear or dislike of advanced technology or complex devices and especially computers." The definition may as well just include my name and photograph.

A scant 30 years ago, I would be writing this column on a typewriter, a device as foreign to my children as their hand-helds are to me. But I am not click-clacking away on my easy, trusty Royal, with sheets of paper crinkled up around my feet like so many giant spitballs. I am instead banging away at the moveable keyboard of my mighty Dell. One false move, one wayward slip of the finger or the hand, and everything I have previously typed can be washed away into oblivion, instead of merely saved as a smear of black ink, easily fixed with White-Out or a crisp new piece of paper.

I often call Kenny in a panic as I struggle to work on my website (connecticutmom.org; I know … shameless plug). I beg for him to help me, to do it for me. And he replies, "You'll never learn if you don't do it yourself." Who the heck is parenting whom?! But what is Greek to me is second nature to him. In a swift and single key stroke, he has made all right with the world. Left to my own devices, the world of technology is a frightening morass of blinking buttons, crossed wires, and shrieking bells and whistles.

I sit amused and amazed as my kids text away on the computer and on their cell phones. Their fingers are so dexterous as they pound away furiously, sending out messages that make no sense to me. Arrangements of letters that actually mean something to their recipients: "OMG!" (Omigod); "IDK!" (I Don't Know); "BBFN" (Bye-bye for Now). Just when I finally got a handle on "LOL" (Laugh Out Loud), Janet and Kenny forbade me from using that in my emails—"Nobody does that anymore, mom!" Even Blake—from far away Iraq—implored me not to insert the yellow smiley faces in my emails anymore: "Die heads, die!" wrote my warrior in an Instant Message. But I loved those yellow smileys! Those were from my generation, dammit! The kids just borrowed them and then promptly deemed them ridiculous. Harumpf!

I have tried texting on my cellphone, but it's farily hopeless. The hardest part is that I ceased being able to read anything smaller than 10-point type about four years ago. In order to actually text I must first find my reading glasses, or hold the flipping phone out from me by about a foot to decipher the letters, and then I can't press the keys hard enough to form a letter, much less a word!

There is a whole generation or so who have never not known a computer to be in the home, nor that phones could be found anywhere but inside a house, or on the occasional street corner, entrapped in a plexiglass box. And then, of course, there are even more generations who have had to adjust to all the new technology, with varying degrees of success and proficiency. I suppose it 'twas ever thus.

It still rattles me though on many levels, the least of which is how ancient and inadequate it can all make me feel at times. Except—a big exception here, I need to remember—that no matter how geeky I may be where computers and cell phones and PDA's are concerned, one doesn't need all of that fancy shmancy stuff to be an effective parent. I still have the lightening fast speed to deny all the fun technology when and if their transgressions allow for that penalty.

"TSSNF (This is so unfair!)" they cry out, devoid of their communication devices, shaking in gadget detoxification.

My response? Well it's as old and as simple as the hills, and can be re-booted as often as I'd like: "HA!"

Yeah. I can do *that!*

InTEXTicated Kids

Tweens and teens texting all over town on their cell phones give new meaning to the phrase, "Thumbs up!"

How do they do it? And how do they do it with such lightening fast speed? Why do they do it instead of just calling? (Probably the same reason most of us resort to email instead of picking up the old-fashioned telephone: it saves time). Somehow in this still-new millennium, the written word speaks faster then, well, the spoken word.

Walking down the street, sitting outside of Starbucks, pulling up in front of the high school or middle school, or the teen center, you will find child upon child with heads bent down towards their cellular devices, thumbs working feverishly. They even *drive* while texting! That seems to be taking things way too far.

Goodness! It was hard enough for me as a teen to learn to type with my *fingers* let alone use my thumbs to send a message on a keyboard as small as a cell phone's. I am a total dork trying to use my thumb to scroll down my contact list with my right thumb, attempting to read the tiny type with my feeble eyes, and then correctly hit send with my left thumb to actually speak. I often mean to call Jon, my husband, but end up hitting "Jen," my friend, instead. Ditto "Hoelzer" instead of "Home." It's a malfunction of eyes *and* digits!

But the kids—yikes! Maybe it's those early years of video game controllers and all of that thumb muscle toning that's built up their dexterity and swiftness. Tap-tap-tap-tap-TAP! Some message or other goes hurtling through the networks of Verizon, Sprint, Cingular and T-Mobile, et al, and just as quickly a response is announced with a tune or a tone.

"Why don't you just call him?" I ask Janet or Jack incredulously. And this generation's answer is always: "Because!"

There is even a service/web site thing called "Twitter," in which you can text dozens of your friends at any given moment: "At the beach," or "Sitting outside of Dunkin' Donuts," or "Going hiking in Colorado." My 22-year-old son, Kenny, does this. I don't get it; who cares? Do all of your friends really need to know what you are doing at any given moment?

The texts I receive from my daughter can be occasionally annoying and suspect. Suspect, especially if I get one during the school day. Annoying, because the text may read: "I have a free in half an hour. Wanna bring me a *$?" (That's shorthand for "Starbucks.") The time I received that particular ditty I texted back: "How 'bout 'No!'"

It is impressive and intimidating and fascinating watching these thumb-typing bandits as they walk, talk, sip beverages, chew gum, snack, and shop, and/or watch TV or school sporting events. It's simply intoxicating for them.

And we're left scratching our heads with our fingers, opposable thumbs clumsy and slow and uncool.

5
SURVIVING SEASONAL HOLIDAYS

Haunt Couture: Giving up the Ghost

"Mom! Why did you dress me like *that* for Halloween?!"

This was Blake's reaction as a 10-year-old upon seeing a photograph taken of him on his first Halloween back in 1983. In the picture he was two months old and I had made a bunny outfit out of an old pillow case. I thought he looked adorable; he thinks he looked like a "geek." My happiest Halloween memories of the kids are from those early days, when I dressed them up in costumes of *my* choosing and making. Take Kenny's first Halloween for example.

Kenny, now 19, was 17-months-old. I had already made a pretty neat costume for Blake—he was going as a construction worker sitting in his bulldozer (a cardboard box painted John Deere yellow and fashioned into a tiny replica of Blake's then favorite piece of machinery). I decided Kenny should trick-or-treat as a pumpkin. I had an orange down-filled ski vest which was suitably puffy and long on my then-toddler, and he wore green pants and a turtleneck, plus a green wool cap with some fake autumn leaves attached to it. I painted his face like a jack-o-lantern. Instant pumpkin costume! Minutes after applying the makeup, he rubbed his hands all over his face, of course, therefore smearing my handiwork and turning him instantly into quite a deranged-looking pumpkin.

I still hold that he looked cute. Years later, seeing the photo of his first big Halloween outing, Kenny is not as amused as I was. "Why didn't you just *buy* me a costume?" he asks.

I upheld family tradition with Janet, now 11, and Jack, 8, creating something memorable for them to don for their first couple of Halloween experiences, but then quickly caved for the next several trick-or-treat adventures with store bought costumes. This year, the costumes are at least partially purchased at a store, and partially scrounged up from stuff around the house. But, sadly, I really miss being costume director. Janet and Jack do not really want my input anymore, so my cute angel and sweet-looking fireman have morphed into a sassy devil and a blood-oozing, sickle wielding skeleton.

It is fun to note how much Halloween brings out the kid even in those far past the age of ringing doorbells with a sack in hand. Three years ago, just after Blake graduated from Marine Corps boot camp, he was home on leave at Halloween. He wanted to go trick-or-treating with the kids and he wanted to "dress up." For him, this meant wearing his newly-issued cammies. (It also means that you, the American tax payer, essentially paid for his Halloween costume!) He had a blast that on that particular All Hallows Eve.

Gone, I suppose, are the days of white sheeted ghosts and pillow cases magically turned into tiny bunnies with the creative cut of a scissor and the tying of a silk ribbon. It's just the mean trick of time. My "Charlie Brown" Halloweens are retired for the time being, yet I will still send my grown-up goblins out next Sunday with a sack and a smile (and I'll probably sport a small tear in my eye as well).

The Spooky Parent

Are you a tricky parent? The constant treat? Or a combination of both? I like being a bit of each, especially at Halloween.

My father loved to scare us at the very last of October. At the dinner table the night before trick-or-treating, he would fake dropping his napkin and then grab one of my brother's or my legs from under the table. We never failed to let out a blood-curdling scream and for years fell for the trick. One year, we hosted a giant kids' Halloween party and my dad was so much more into it than any of the three dozen pre-teens assembled in their ghoulish finest. He hid behind doors and popped out, donned a hideous mask, and stood still as stone in a darkened hallway. He forced our guests to place their hands inside a bowl with peeled grapes and cold as ice spaghetti ("The monster's eyeballs and guts," he'd cackle wildly). Creepy. Yet loveable.

I recall as a kid how much more fun a house was to beg for—whoops!—I mean *trick-or-treat* for candy, if the mom or dad answered the door dressed in costume. My friends and I would feel a tad tentative in spite of ourselves, yet we'd thoroughly enjoy the little "show" the person of the adult persuasion would put on for our benefit.

For the past four years friends and neighbors of ours hold a Halloween-themed birthday party for the oldest son, a good friend of my kid, Jack. The parents transform their basement into a first-rate haunted house, always with a different theme (classic Halloween hair-raising the first year, then pirate the next. Last year was ghastly ghoulish and this year has a zombie-like focus). They ask me to dress up appropriately to greet the party guests.

That first year I donned a Grim Reaper get-up and only the birthday boy and Jack knew that it was me inside the black robe and mask, eyes eerily blinking a blood red behind a face-covered cloak. It was oddly amusing scaring the pants out of the little boys as they arrived. By the second year, however, return invitees muttered a nonchalant, "Hi, Mrs. Evans," while the virgin guests slightly cowered before someone clued them in as to whom that masked (wo)man really was. No matter; it is still entertaining.

The host's mother also gets into the spirit with an appropriate costume of her own, her husband reigns scarily supreme inside the haunted house, and I think the kids are fine with the fact that Halloween seems to be just as enjoyable for the grown-ups. Our role as a parent can mostly be seen by children as too serious, so it's important for them to see once in a while that we also know how to let our hair and guard down, and if only for one spooky night become more friend than foe.

As the years have gone by my children have turned more jaded about my enthusiasm for the rituals of All Hallows Eve. Teenager Janet chided me last year, *"Really?* How old are you?" as I left for the birthday party in full monstrous regalia. This year both seem uncertain about my decorating the yard with some chilling October 31st night paraphernalia. They are getting older, but that doesn't mean I necessarily have to acknowledge my own increase in years of living.

You're only as old as you feel. So, I'm about 12 every October. Now that's a slightly scary thought!

An Attitude of Gratitude

We are about to enter the season of "gimme." And so, I suggest that tomorrow, as you gather 'round the dining room table for turkey and such, that you ask your children—no matter how wee or how wise—what they are thankful for and why. This suggestion may seem obvious.

At our table, we ask and we answer. From the younger two, the thanks is almost always about a thing—a toy or a piece of electronics. At age 20, Kenny can now point to more emotional or socially-based concepts for which he is grateful, such as graduating from college, securing a job, finding an apartment. Blake, the U.S. Marine, has not been home for Thanksgiving in four years, which may be the very thing for which he is thankful on a 22-year-old level!

My husband Jon and I are usually predictable in our giving of thanks: we are always happy to have the family together, to have our collective health, to have our children alive (Blake in particular, given his career).

My father died nine years ago yesterday, on the anniversary of John F. Kennedy's death. With it falling so precariously close to Thanksgiving, there is always a part of me that does not feel very thankful, because I miss him and feel he was taken away way too soon. And now my mother is also absent. This will be the first Thanksgiving in my entire life where I will find myself unable to either see or speak with any parent. The urge to dwell in self-pity looms large, except when I remember that I should remain grateful that I had as much time with them as was allowed. My own children don't need to see me blubber all over my stuffing and gravy. They need to see me smile and they need me to love them—and be grateful, too, for that.

This year, though, I want to try something different, something beyond the verbal giving of thanks: I am going to ask them to write a gratitude list.

A gratitude list can comprise *things,* material possessions, but it should moreover include personal physical attributes we are grateful for (long hair, strong legs, blue eyes). Also, people in our lives, such as parents, best friends, a teacher, a dog or cat (okay, dogs and cats are technically not people, but …), and traits about home that both children and adults may not often think about being grateful for. For instance, a pond in the backyard, three windows in the bedroom, a good sledding hill, or a cool playroom. A gratitude list may also feature certain qualities about us that equal giving—being a good friend, the ability to make someone laugh when they are feeling sad, and offering helpful advice.

Children should be reminded that giving equals getting and that the getting isn't always something that they can hold in their hands or wear or watch. That they can give one of those items to others without expecting or wanting anything back but a "thank you," whether audible or silent.

From Thanksgiving until Christmas and/or Hanukah, the life of a child is usually about the gimme's; the getting. Yet as the saying goes in some circles, "You can't keep it unless you give it away." The "it" isn't a physical thing, like a toy truck, a video game or a doll. The "it" is gratitude for being able to help another. It is going from entitled to appreciative, and an un-entitled child is just one more thing for which to be thankful.

Weighty Issues

"Your butt looks so cute in your football pants," I remarked to Jack recently. "The pads make it stick out!" To which he replied, "Well you don't need football pads for your butt to stick out, fatty!" What a sweet child. I'm hoping he was joking.

Janet and Jack also like to swing my upper arm flab back and forth privately and—cringingly enough—in public as well. I bat them off with a stern "stop it," but it's hilarious to them. Reminiscent of naughty two-year-olds, they persist, as if my physical shortcoming were some kind of fun plaything to flick.

I've earned my wobbly bits, both through birthing four children (that's a positive), and through devouring about 4,000 pints of Ben&Jerry's (that's not so positive, but they have been very tasty). And now we're entering the Bermuda triangle of eating—Thanksgiving, Christmas and New Year's. The winter padding season begins tomorrow!

Like many women, I struggle with body image, something I've done ever since my father remarked to me in the eighth grade that if I continued to snack I'd end up looking like my mother, who at the time, was going through an overweight period. That comment was enough to do it; "it" being making me as a teen and 20-something hyper-aware of what I ate and how thin I looked. Comments such as that can and do affect countless young teenage girls, who—during the middle school years especially—begin to compare their bodies to both their peers and models or celebrities.

Boys, too, have their own tussles with what their bodies are doing, or in some cases, *not* doing. They want to be taller, stronger. Even at age 10, Jack has only feebly tried out my free weights, which is more than fine with me. There's plenty of time for bicep building down the line. Be 10, have pencil arms, it's alright. Blake, now 23, was the scrawniest, gangliest thing around in middle and early high school. Then he began sprouting muscles and today he's a hulk and a hunk.

Girls identify with thin and boys with bulk, vertically or horizontally. Both want to be taller or shorter, sleeker or muscular. But there isn't much one can do about genes, and therefore, your jeans are going to fit the body your mamma gave you. That fact can be hard to swallow, however.

As parents, we need to try and watch the messages we send, chiefly to our daughters. I have been blameworthy for commenting woefully on my own backside in Janet's presence and moaning about how "fat" I am. Conversely, I am also quick to nip in the bud her own evaluation of her legs, tummy, etc. when she begins picking herself apart and threatening not to eat (which thankfully hasn't happened). It is a "yet" that I hope we can avoid. Her father and I need to keep reminding her of how great she looks, whether extra pounds eventually find her or not.

I'd like to think that in spite of my own disparaging comments regarding my body, that she notices her father has loved me literally through thick and thin, and that I haven't lost any friends regardless of what weight I gain. That I am Julie, no matter what the scale or blue jeans say to the outside world. And that she will always be sweet Janet.

Actress Kirstie Alley recently remarked to Oprah (after appearing in a bikini on her show), that "we aren't our bodies." It's what's inside our bodies that ultimately weigh in with the world.

Chew on that thought tomorrow. Happy Thanksgiving!

Happy Thankmasoween!

Is it just me, or is the holiday trilogy of Halloween-Thanksgiving-Christmas blending frighteningly into one confusing lump? And how is that affecting our children's view that Halloween, Thanksgiving and Christmas/Chanukah are really distinct, separate celebrations?

Here it is, the day before Thanksgiving, and hardly any fanfare was paid to this totally American holiday in stores or in the media. Any turkey day decorations were seemingly and clumsily displayed for about 19 seconds on November 1st and then relegated to the back storage rooms in retail stores. Why? I'll tell you why—because this holiday doesn't include the mass purchasing of toys or clothing or costumes for kids. One need only buy food products, and not in fine stores everywhere, but purely in supermarkets. In our kid-centric world, Thanksgiving doesn't sell. It ain't sexy, folks.

This, despite the fact that Thanksgiving is perhaps the quintessential, American family holiday.

Back-to-School: That's kid-friendly by far. The displays and reminders begin to pop into retail stores in late July. By mid-August, even though our family is still out in Wyoming, even though it is still summer, the kids begin to query as to when we can go "back-to-school shopping." *Really*? Enjoy the freaking heat and sunshine and no school, I want to shout. There's plenty of time left! We can buy a few pencils the day before school starts and do the rest later! Thousands, nay millions, of us grew up on that theory and we're none the worse for wear.

And seemingly two days after that first day of school, in stores such as CVS, out come the ceramic pumpkins, and humongous bags of candy and costumes, sitting side-by-side with the dwindling displays of notebooks and locker-ladders. Then—Boom! Like clockwork, my children would start (*still* start in spite of the fact that the younger two are now 11 and 14) to request my purchasing them a mask or wig or cape, et al, for Halloween. A holiday that is still at least six to seven weeks away.

The candy corn is barely digesting in all of our bellies, the jack-o-lanterns aren't yet rotting, and…. Ta-da! It's time for Halloween displays to be grudgingly set aside and out come the evergreen and holly and toys and the sounds of Christmas Carols(!) wafting through the air, assaulting all of our senses. What happened to the brief lull between Halloween and Christmas?!

The season of "gimmes" begins far too early for kids. As recently as my older boys' childhoods (they are now 22 and 24, respectively) there was still a clear break between trick-or-treating and holiday greeting. The doorbell rang on the last day of October and candy was given out. In late December, the doorbell rang and a gaily-wrapped gift was presented. But between the holidays of "gets" was the blessedly simple, altruistic celebration of thanks. It was more the calm-before-the-storm of the December festivals. Sure, the day after Thanksgiving—Black Friday—officially kicks off the consumerism frenzy. But we used to be eased into that with more grace (pardon the pun).

Just one week after Halloween this year, my son, Jack, presented me with his Christmas wish list. Horrified, although not entirely surprised, given the fact that December 25th decorations were ostensibly everywhere, I accepted it. And quickly tossed it into the "to do" pile of papers. Papers that I don't plan to address until mid-December, when traditionally I enter into the Christmas spirit. *Hello!* We still have Thanksgiving to attend to.

Although anxiety-laced with meal preparation and projection of certain relatives behaving badly, Thanksgiving is—or should be—a day where not only is Halloween a distant memory and Christmas anticipation yet to be thrust into, but a day of family bonding. A day to recognize the genius of the pilgrims and a celebration of all there is to be grateful. A time to truly be hopeful of twinkly lights appearing soon on trees and across front porches, and of the thick-as-telephone-book Toys R' Us catalog arriving in the mail. It should not be an occasion to drive over the river and through the woods to grandma's house passing by garish lighting already in place, and seeing evergreen trees strapped to vehicle's roofs.

I am thankful that even though my younger two are gift-list crazed, they are also bewildered by the premature Christmassizing of America. It's a small victory in my desire to try and keep them focused on one festivity at a time. That each is precious—and separate—no matter how hard some national retailers try to convince the collective us otherwise.

As a *Time* magazine columnist recently pointed out, George Bernard Shaw said it best: "A perpetual holiday is a good working definition of hell." Thanks, George!

Yes, Jack, there is a Santa Claus

*(Writer's note: With much credit and apologies
to newsman Francis P. Church, circa 1897)*

Last Christmas brought with it the question about Santa, just as it had done three preceding times before. It made the holidays especially bittersweet as the baby of the family took his place Christmas morn with his older siblings, four sets of eyes filled with a little less magic. My heart heaved. The reign was over. Or was it? Santa Claus or no Santa Claus?

Jack, your little friends were wrong. They have been affected by the skepticism of a cynical and electronically charged age. They do not believe except (what) they see online, on television and in the movies. They think that nothing can be which is not comprehensible by their little minds.

Yes, Jack, there is a Santa Claus. Who else would sprinkle that magic dust on you and Janet, Kenny and Blake? Who but Santa would leave that same shower of fine and twinkly silver on the hearth? Santa exists certainly as love and generosity and devotion exist, and you know that they abound and give to your life its highest beauty and joy. (No—video games and computers and balls of all shapes and sizes should not be what give you your highest joy.) Alas! How dreary would be the world if there were no Santa Claus! It would be as dreary as if there were no Jacks. And if there were no Jacks, there would be no childlike faith then, no Mother's Day poetry and no random pats on my back to make this existence tolerable. With no Jacks, we should have no enjoyment, except in sense and sight. The eternal light which childhood fills the world be extinguished.

Not believe in Santa Claus! You might as well not believe in the ghosts of Babe Ruth and Lou Gehrig! You might get dad to hire men to watch all the chimneys in New Canaan on Christmas Eve to catch Santa Claus, or get Blake to stand guard in green and red cammies, but even if they did not see Santa Claus coming down, what would that prove? Nobody sees Santa Claus. The most real things in the world are those that neither children nor men (or women!) can see. Did you ever see Babe or Lou dancing in the outfield or by the plate, ready to help you hit a homer or catch a fly ball? Of course not, but that's no proof that they are not here. Nobody can conceive or imagine all the wonders of the world there are unseen and unseeable in the world.

You tear apart the baby's rattle and see what makes the noise inside, but there is a veil covering the unseen world which not the strongest man, nor even the united strength of all the strongest men that ever lived, could tear apart. Ah, Jack—No Santa Claus! Thank God he lives and he lives forever. A thousand years from now, nay, ten times ten thousand years from now, he will continue to make glad the heart of childhood.

You can Google him and think you have the proof, you can sneak around my closets this month, you can smirk in the malls at the helper Claus, but you will never discover tangible evidence of his non-existence. For he is in your heart, your memory; in the unseen, magical December air. And he's as close as that soft kiss on your cheek while you sleep.

So don't pout and please don't shout. Santa is *so* comin' to town.

The Best Christmas Gift

For several Christmases now, I haven't made a long list of items that I would like to receive from my husband or my children. Like many adults, I am blessed to be able to afford most things that I would like or need, and so I much prefer working with Santa on the giving part. To paraphrase: "It is in the giving that we receive."

You don't have to be a grown-up to understand the gifts in giving. Recently, a first grader was inspired to sell hundreds of chocolate bears from a school fundraiser for the children affected by Hurricane Katrina. My eight-year-old niece, Noelle, who lives in Jackson Hole, Wyoming, forgoes receiving birthday presents, and instead asks her party guests to contribute to a charity. These children—and many others like them—"get" the giving.

I'm sure I am not unlike other parents who find a giddy joy in watching their children's faces on Christmas morn as they discover and open gifts that were included on their wish lists. I also love the look of surprise and sincere thanks on the face of my husband when he opens a hoped-for item. The hugs, the wet kisses on my cheek, the squeals of "I love you, mommy" from my adolescent daughter, and the "Cool! Thanks, mom and Jon," from Kenny are priceless (although Jon might disagree on the "priceless" part once the credit card bill comes in!).

For three Christmases in a row now, since 2002, there has been an absent "thank-you" and presence in our living room. There is a stocking that has been faithfully hung and filled, only to have the contents packaged up on December 26, and sent thousands of miles away. I hear a "Thanks, Mom," over the telephone, but I have longed to see the dimpled cheeks, and receive a holiday hug from well-toned and trained, battle-ready arms attached to my oldest child.

But this year will be different. This Christmas I am getting the best gift of all—four children by the tree. By the time this column is printed I will have greeted the missing piece of my present and driven it home from the Jet Blue terminal at JFK airport: My very own Rambo will return for the holidays.

Blake emailed me recently to inquire as to what I would like for Christmas. My answer, of course, was nothing; his being home is the gift.

Children grow up. They leave the nest and settle elsewhere, marry, maybe reproduce, and come back home when schedules allow. Beliefs grow out, and for the first time in 22 years, I will not be up into the wee hours, nor woken up in them either. I will mourn that this year, yet I know that ritual will come again down the line, when my children have their own children and accept our invitation to spend the holidays with us here at home.

Children cherish what they get on December 25th, and they don't even realize, yet, that they cherish what they give as well; the laughter, the palatable appreciation, the hunkering down for the day with family. We know that comes later, when the things aren't as important as the "thing." That *thing* being the original reason this holiday is celebrated, as well as being together with parents and siblings.

Since 2002 I have felt incomplete on Christmas morning and it is obvious as to why. But this year I will once again have the first gift of the day in the twilight of morning as child after child after child after child piles into our bed before heading down to the boxes, bows, bags, and toys in the living room.

Thank you, Santa, in advance.

Holiday Hysteria and Managing the Madness

When I picture my oldest child Blake, now 21, at his first walking and talking Christmas, it is of a 16-month-old roaring about my then in-law's apartment with candy canes in each hand, and a face streaked with sticky red sugar. His excitement was both tangible and aromatic, and colorful bows and papers were flung madly with the abandon only the young can muster.

Other holiday memories include a five-year-old Kenny projectile vomiting all over his stash from Santa, as well as a three-year-old Janet screaming bloody murder at having to be whisked away from a line to see Santa, because her then baby brother Jack (only eight months old at the time) had been accidentally dropped on his head by her uncle, suffering a fractured skull. Ah, the holidays. Fun stuff.

Containing a child's joy is difficult at this time of year and is not necessarily something a parent should attempt. They are allowed and expected to be full of awe and wonder. Yet they know that the getting of gifts, toys and such looms large. They can be consumed with, well, consuming. The "I wants" can get out-of-control. Reigning that in is tricky, but important business for parents.

How many times have you uttered: "The holidays are a time of giving, not just getting" to your six-year-old? Does your four-year-old point and scream at the sight of a "must-have" toy at the store, and you need to gracefully or not-so-gracefully exit the store as he/she wails and flails? Has your 10-year-old presented you with a list that resembles the inventory of Radio Shack (cell phone, lap-top, MP-3 player, video game system, digital camera)?

Encouraging your child to do for others at this time of year (actually throughout the year) is what will help them to adopt a more giving, and a less getting, attitude. Donating their outgrown toys and clothes to a shelter or to the visiting Goodwill truck is one way to help them realize that not everybody is as fortunate. One holiday season five years ago Blake, who used to work at the local market, drove me, Janet and Jack to the homeless shelter with a huge bag of bagels and donuts that had been left over for the residents to enjoy.

I've also found that having the kids use their own allowance to purchase a gift or two reminds them of sacrifice and giving of your own. We also have padded that allowance by $20 or so to let them experience staying and buying within a budget.

Each year that our family seems to lose a believer, that child is then allowed to help be an elf before bedtime on Christmas Eve. It has actually been just as special and as poignant a time as is the Christmas morning's absolute jaw-dropping, face full of wonderment moment of discovery that the big jolly guy has visited the house. The experience of being the giver—to me and to them—is far more satisfying and meaningful than being the recipient of a well-wrapped box.

The real meaning of the season, however, was admittedly and embarrassingly and temporarily lost on me a couple of years ago.

On Christmas Eve in '02, I walked Jack and Janet around town after the candle light celebration at our church. We spoke about the origin of Christmas, and I purposely took them over to the Catholic Church's nativity scene downtown. We chatted briefly about the first Christmas and the baby Jesus. But the baby Jesus was not in the manger!

"Oh my goodness," I said to the kids. "Somebody stole the baby Jesus! Who would do that?" I spotted a patrol car across the street, and grabbed the kids' hands as we dashed over to the officer. I was doing a good deed on Christmas Eve, I thought, showing the kids about caring and such.

"Officer," I panted. "Somebody has stolen the baby Jesus!" He smiled politely and reported that he would look into it, and wished us a happy holiday.

We came home and I felt full of goodwill, if not also a bit shocked that someone would vandalize the crèche. I immediately told my husband and the older boys about our discovery.

"Can you believe somebody took the baby Jesus?" I asked incredulously. The three males broke out laughing.

"You idiot," my husband replied sort of kindly. "Of course there's no baby Jesus in there! He's not born until Christmas day!"

Oh. Yeah. I knew that.

So much for being the "expert." But at least I taught the younger kids a lesson in humility during the holidays. And unexpectedly added to some family holiday lore.

Holiday Magic Family-style

"It's the most wonderful time of the year," goes the Christmas carol. And a time of miracles, big and small.

December holidays celebrate the miraculous birth of Jesus, the astonishing, eight-day burning of olive oil as witnessed by the Macabees. And, of course, there is the magic of Santa Claus.

People are for the most part cheerier. Some gladly give up a coveted parking spot for others in the spirit of the season. Others calmly wait in lines they would ordinarily be squirming and griping in. Those who would otherwise feel entitled, instead employ grace and patience. Magic.

Last week while waiting at a stop light, I watched a mother viewing the church's crèche with her toddler son in her arms, gesturing animatedly as her child stared at the scene wide-eyed and reverent. Magic.

In early December, a friend shared a story about her child's first Hanukah, of how delighted her young daughter was to light a candle each evening, and—of course—how thrilling it was to receive a special gift for eight days running. The little girl embraced her religion with respect beyond her young years.

At the mall I choked up observing tiny children eyeing Santa with the worship usually reserved for rock starts. Their belief was contagious and tangible, belying this century's fast-paced, "Miracles. *Really?*," attitude. Magic.

Although families observe and carry out traditions all year 'round, those employed during the holiday season are especially poignant: The trips into New York for a holiday show or a visit to Rockefeller Center; cutting down your own tree; annual parties attended by every member of the family. Perhaps there is a pilgrimage to a homeless shelter to help spread joy, or a special dessert on Christmas Eve, or caroling in the cold air.

I always find my children's participation in family traditions year after year—especially as they grow—to be somewhat nothing short of astonishing.

From tots to teens to 20-somethings, they continue to cooperate in the ritual of hanging their own ornaments on the tree (each gets a new one every year), to being a Santa's helper, to piling into our bed on the morning of the 25th, to making the pancake and egg breakfast on Christmas after opening gifts. And, oh yeah, keeping quiet during mom's late morning nap. Any other day of the year there is bound to be noise, but on December 25th, the nap is pure bliss!

My kids are now older and a bit jaded during the rest of the year. But as Christmas nears the moody pre-teen and teenager, the battle and/or travel-worn, sport a seasonal light in their eyes and in their step; it is precious. Secrets are kept, presents are cleverly hidden by both parent and child, smiles appear or re-appear more readily, and they seem to be a bit nicer to me and their dad. Of course that could also be a ploy for us to fulfill their every Christmas wish. Regardless, I will take the magic and the pleasantness any which way it comes.

We all still speak with awe of the Christmas Eve the colored lights decorating an outdoor pine turned on without the benefit of electricity, signaling the presence of a ghost of holidays past. It was December of 1996; one month after my father had died. At the time, we were living in the house in which I had grown up and had recently purchased from my parents. My dad had strung lights on a tree by the front of the house years before and kept them up—as did we—throughout the year, plugging them in only at Christmastime. But during December of 1996 they did not turn on and we blamed it on ancient wiring finally gone badly.

On Christmas Eve, still keen with grief, I walked into the living room to place some gifts under the tree, feeling leaden with both the sadness of loss, and the burden of having to quell that in the presence of my children. As I stood up and glanced outside, the lights on the pine tree sprung to life. My eyes darted back to the plug that was strung through the living room window to the outdoors, but it lay dormant on the floor. My heart raced as I screamed for my family to look out the window. They dashed in and I queried my husband about having perhaps plugged the extension cord in from another location. He shook his head "no" as he put his arm around my shoulder and all of us stared with wonder at the scene outside the window.

"It's grandpa," whispered Blake, then 13, both solemn and elated.

I choked back tears as best I could. "It's grandpa alright," I said.

Blake and Kenny dashed outside for a closer look, and returned with cheeks flushed from both the chill and the thrill.

"It's magic!" Kenny cried, hugging me.

"A Christmas miracle," I replied, smiling, yet stunned. Magic indeed.

Resolution Solutions

New Year's Resolutions are pretty much made to broken. There are good intentions behind them—or at least behind some of them. While the naming of behavior-changing objectives at the start of a new year is a good lesson for both parent and child, it's the follow-through in which the true lesson lies.

Here are some of my resolutions for this coming year:

For my eldest child, Blake, I resolve to: Breathe and wait patiently—or as patiently as I can muster—when weeks go by without an email. I resolve to stop bugging him every other email about purchasing a cell phone that works internationally, so that he can call me from his base in far off Okinawa. I additionally resolve to cease inquiring as to whether or not a marriage is in his future. Experiencing grandchildren before I am too much older, grayer and less spry would be really nice, but I will zip my lip in 2008 (I can't promise the same for 2009 however).

For my 22-year-old son Kenny, I resolve to: Keep remembering that he is just 22 and not necessarily ready to settle down with a "real" job. *Any* job is preferable right now, but I resolve to gently remind him of that fact, not get right in his face. The urge to lay a gigantic motherly guilt trip on his young self is strong to tremendous, yet I will endeavor to position such a trip in a more tactful, less obvious manner. I additionally resolve to resist contacting him the nano-second something goes awry with my computer or I-Touch or other such similar electronic, technological device.

For my daughter, Janet, I resolve to: Be less judgmental of certain actions and fashions. I may not agree with the whys, but I will try and let her be her, whatever the metamorphosis entails this freshman year. I will also be extra careful about using words and phrases more appropriate for a teen than a middle-aged mother of four. Slang like "whatevs," "kickin'," "word up" and "hooking up." (To me, "hooking up" means meeting with someone, but apparently in teen-dom it means something altogether less innocent.)

For youngest child, Jack, a sixth grader, I resolve to: Stop asking him if he has a girlfriend, quit reminding him to do his homework while he is in the midst of doing it (only to me it doesn't look as if he is since the television is on), and bring an end to playfully requesting he score a dozen points for me in his basketball games. I didn't realize he took that silly suggestion to heart, and the parental pressure was a pain, to say the least. Of course, I hope he resolves to lighten up and recognize a joke when he hears one!

Kids should make resolutions too, even if they last but a day or a week or a month. Everyone has area for improvement, even those who are still in the process of growing, maturing and finding their way in the world.

"Stick to your guns," "Follow through on your responsibilities," and "Finish what you started," aren't simply annoying parental axioms. They are time honored and often-tested truths that we can all benefit from on the journey to becoming better, more service oriented, more self-esteemed human beings.

In terms of much uttered wise suggestions, though, lies the ever-popular, "Do as I say, not as I do." If you're going to state a resolution, model to your kids that you can actually execute it.

I resolve to resolve that oft-unresolved suggestion. How about you?

6
HOT FUN IN THE SUMMERTIME?

Trippin' with the Kids

Summer seems pretty much synonymous with family vacations, whether it's Vermont or Venice; the Jersey Shore or the shores of France; the Wild West or the Mid-East; Nantucket or Newport News. We grab our kids and evacuate for days or weeks, leaving our hometown streets strewn with tumbleweeds—a ghost town.

Okay, so I exaggerate a tad. But summer is travel time, so wherever you're going and whatever your child's age, remember that a family vacation should be enjoyed by all members of the family. In other words, consider the ages of your children when choosing your destination and your expectations of their appreciation.

We are very fortunate to have recently visited my husband's mother, who happens to live in northern Cyprus; the Turkish side of the island. My husband had visited there numerous times pre-marriage, but the kids and I had never ventured to their grandmother's house. While fascinating for me to see this culture and ancient ruins and mosques, the kids were mostly happy to stay at grandma's house and swim in the pool. We did venture out, of course, and Jack was more excited about exploring the 3,000-year-old castles than was Janet, but she was a trooper nonetheless (until she spotted lizards the size of puppies and ran screaming down one castle's crumbling steps in leaps and bounds).

On our way back to the States, we stayed in Rome for three nights, and here is where the agenda of parent and child collided in the hot, steamy Italian sun. With no in-depth education about ancient Rome under their belts, the kids were duly unimpressed with the Coliseum, Vatican City and the Palladium. Janet mostly wanted to ogle the windows of Gucci, Versace and Prada. Jack yearned to check out gelato stands and purchase a Team Italia soccer jersey. Each time Jon would tell us that this pizza restaurant or that gelato place or that some church he read about in the tour guide book was "really close," we wound up walking block upon block, hungry and parched, longing to dive into any old vat of gelato, guide-book blessed or not.

I know that as my children age and their classes inform each more of this spectacular and history-steeped city, they will appreciate having been among its columns and Basilicas and obelisks. As it was, though, we hadn't considered that our idea of touring and theirs were pretty different, and walking miles in the scorching sun would be easier for us then for them. I was insistent that they not remember Rome as the place where daddy made them sweat and be bored by old buildings.

Even staying closer to home for a trip should mean remembering that it's everybody's vacation, not just mom and dad's. Let the kids plan the agenda one day, even if that means eating ice cream for breakfast, playing mini-golf three times in a row and building enough sand castles to populate a small city.

As a single parent in the early 1990's, I took Blake and Kenny to Disney World when they were young, and pretty much let them make the call on which rides to experience and which park to attend each day. I guided them to Space Mountain, Pirates of the Caribbean, and other classic Disney adventures that I knew of from previous trips, but I realized that it was really a vacation about what *they* wanted, not what I really wished I could be doing (lounging by a pool, avoiding lines, eating fruit instead of cotton candy …). That adventure is still fondly remembered.

Some down time on any holiday is welcomed by both young and old, so try not to schedule every moment of every day. Occasionally a trip is best remembered for the spontaneous discovery. And, very often, the best touring a family can do is the one of exploring each other.

"I'm Bored!" What Happened to Summertime Fun?

Okay, summer has only just begun and if I hear the phrase, "I'm bored," uttered from anyone under the age of 15 again any time soon, I don't know what I'll do, but it won't be pleasant. Yes, I know that even I, as a child, whined those same two words. But I don't believe I said them as often, and certainly not in the face of so much stimulation.

As a kid growing up in the woods of Connecticut, I had plenty to explore on hot summer days—streams, large boulders, dense forest, great tree-climbing trees. I could also ride my bicycle along what seemed to be miles and miles of fairly car-less roads and lanes. My friends and I all knew how to make forts from branches and rocks. As I became older, perhaps 11 or 12, my girlfriends and I would walk to one another's houses or hang out at the small shopping center, seeking out the lurking boys.

In the absence of air conditioning, we knew how to cool ourselves off with ice cubes smoothed over the inside of our wrists. I read *a lot*. Watching television during the day was unheard of unless you were a grandma who was hooked on "the stories," i.e. soap operas.

Whatever did we do without: TV; VCR's; DVD players; Game Boys; X-Box; computers; ornate playsystems; basketball hoops on paved driveways; large pitching and hitting nets … You get the picture. Whatever did we do? Read above.

The year 2004 is light years away in many respects from 1964. I wish I could feel more comfortable letting my kids roam the nearby woods, but there's the big tick scare and reality of Lyme disease. Although my mother let us dart about the trees for hours, I'd probably be afraid that Jack or Janet would get lost, or worse, kidnapped. And it's a fear that these days is well-founded.

I encouraged Jack to make a clubhouse out of the little "fort" that is part of our wooden swing-set. I was met with a blank stare.

"What are you talking about," he asked. "How do you do *that?!*"

I explained that he could sweep out the cobwebs, put some plastic furniture up there, make a list of rules for the "club" with some friends, and maybe sleep out there one hot night with his buddy Cole. He was less than enthusiastic about the whole plan.

My daughter, Janet, is the queen of moaning about how bored she is. Self-entertaining is not her forte'. "Read!" I scream at her, to which she rolls her eyes and declares that reading is too much like school and it is summer vacation. I wordlessly point to the stack of summer reading books she insisted that I purchase and walk away.

It is not my job to entertain my children. If they are bored, it is *their* fault. They need to use their imagination the way I and countless others did before the days of multi-media and instant gratification.

Although the world is less safe than it once was, they can still pop outside and check out nature. We can all walk the trails at the town park or the nature center, and I can even let them run on ahead, feeling free and independent.

When I ignore their pleas for excitement from a manufactured source, I will soon hear the sounds of a game of tag being played or hide-and-go-seek. Jack will try and capture a frog from our pond and Janet will turn cartwheels on the lawn. They will even play catch together.

My kids may never—will never—have the kind of summers that I once did, but I am hoping that they can leave behind the "I'm bored" phase, and replace it with actions that don't come with instructions, a plug, or a joystick. I'll let you know in September if the mission was accomplished!

Kids, the Country and Freedom

Yesterday we celebrated the Fourth of July, the birth of our nation and all that freedom stands for. Every year, I am hoping that my children gain a keener understanding that the initial freedom of these United States of America wasn't "free," and that even today, there is a price.

Given the times in which they are living—especially in the years since September 11, 2001—and the older brother who took an oath to "support and defend the Constitution of the United States against all enemies foreign and domestic," I believe they are getting the gist.

The kids have been fortunate enough to have visited London, Paris and Rome (that sounds like they're some upscale store, doesn't it?), as well the Mediterranean, the place their Evans' grandmother calls home. These trips have provided a taste, a peek, into other cultures and customs outside of their own, and have perhaps supplied a growing appreciation of the differences between our country and others. But I think a good look at some of the United States is in order for them as well.

Two summers ago, I loaded up the car with Janet, now 14, and Jack, now 11, and drove from Connecticut out to Wyoming, where Janet has been attending camp, and where we spend a chunk of the summer each year. Primarily we saw more amber waves of grain then we cared to, until we reached the purple mountain majesty of which we are already familiar. I dashed so fast across the Midwest that they really didn't get much of a taste for what lies between sea to shining sea.

This year I hope to allow for more than a snippet of America.

At the start of next week Janet, a friend of hers from camp, my son Kenny, 22, and I will climb into my SUV in search of America. (Actually, we are driving back out to Wyoming to pick Jack up from camp and deliver Janet to same camp for her session. We will then kick back in Jackson Hole for a month). But a good part of America will be searched! I want the kids to see that the diversity of America isn't only present in the landscape, but also in her citizens.

I'd like to have a leisurely lunch near Pennsylvania Dutch country, so that they might see an Amish village, a buggy, or a Lancaster County family up close. To witness in the flesh that not all teenage girls feel a need to, nor can they, dress head-to-toe in Abercrombie, Hollister or Ralph Lauren. Stop for gas and a soda in Illinois, catching a few rays of sun beside a corn field where somebody's father works the land with nary a Blackberry in sight. Kenny and I want to drive down a piece of the infamous Route 66, starting probably from south of Chicago and then continue through part of Kansas. And then we'll ramble back up north towards the Rockies and our destination state.

On the drive back, with just Janet and Jack as passengers, I hope to take another meandering, spacious skies route and visit Mt. Rushmore and the Badlands, then veer off into a bit of Wisconsin and Minnesota, before heading back across the fruited plains and the final density of New England.

"Turn off the DVD player, kids," I will exclaim. "Look out the windows! Look at America the beautiful! We are so lucky to live here!" This is the land of the free and of the brave. This is the country that was and will always be worth fighting for. It is the country that young men and women have died and will continue dying for, if they choose to join our armed forces.

"Don't be afraid," I will also tell them. "That doesn't mean your brother Blake will die, too, but if … if God forbid he did … it will be because freedom isn't free, but it still merits defense whether it's on our soil or another's."

My children already know from history lessons and from current events that not all wars make sense, that America's involvement in battles isn't always clear and evident. Yet I want them to also understand that a country that values liberty and justice for all is a precious place in which to live, and that it is worth preserving. As corny as it may sound, I hope for them to be proud citizens.

If I can show them as much of their country as is physically and financially possible, then maybe they'll have a fuller picture. After driving through a dusty desert town without a national retailer or a fast-food chain in sight, maybe they'll not take for granted the area in which they live. A big home in a leafy suburb of New York City, filled with state-of-the-art electronic devices isn't a right; it's a privilege that must be appreciated.

Life, liberty and the pursuit of happiness. We give these to our children at their birth and all we can anticipate is their understanding for, and of, the latter two. The search for the source is priceless.

Slow Down and Savor Summer

"Summertime … and the living is easy," go the song lyrics. But is it? Can you and your children slow it down enough so that you can really savor summer?

We are so programmed to go-go-go that it may be difficult to allow unstructured, less hurried moments during July and August. Many times our kids career straight from a full school day to a full camp day or, if old enough, a full-time summer job. And as parents we are just as frenzied in getting our offspring to and from their next activity or responsibility.

There's a new slogan in town, appearing on car magnets and street signs that reads: "Slow Down in Our Town." The slogan refers to driving, of course, but I needed that simple life reminder this morning … Instead I got a very expensive reminder.

As I bopped along in my convertible on a bright, sunny, summer morning to meet a friend for a walk, I noticed that the time on my dashboard read "8:27;" we were meeting at 8:30. I am a prompt person, having been raised by very prompt parents. Every bone in my body screamed: "Be there by 8:30!" I was driving by the entrance to the baseball park and decided to put some more pressure on my gas pedal, so as to arrive at the nature trails at the appointed hour. As if my friend, Wendy, would have vanished if I pulled in at 8:32 instead of the stroke of 8:30. No sooner had I slammed into third gear than one of my town's finest flagged over one of town's fastest. Busted!

Was my rush worth an infraction costing upwards of $100? Absolutely not. Did Wendy care that I showed up at 8:40 (looking very sheepish and chastised)? Again, absolutely not.

Slowing down for life—for summer—is a good, healthy thing. Slow doesn't always equal lazy or rude or low ambition. Easy does it, but do it. That's the ticket, no pun intended.

Believe me, I know keenly that near-feeling of dread when summer yawns large and I fear I will be the primary source of entertainment and transportation for my kids. There's the choking sensation that my summer will mean no down time, and that I need to be here and there, and there and here, just as I am during the school year. In the past I have signed my kids up for day camps, half-day camps, week long morning programs, something, anything so that they won't turn to and on me. And, in my selfishness, I may have deprived them of time for themselves.

When we have time on our hands, we can create, we can grow, we can learn. In our boredom—in our child's "boredom"—much can be discovered. About how and what we feel, what we fear and what we fear not. With the sun beating down and the low din of crickets in the fields, or sounds of the laps of water upon a beach, or the trickle of a stream through a wood, our thoughts can produce great insight and knowing.

Children need structure but also the lack thereof, if only for a few weeks in the summer; it makes the time all the more savory. They make memories out of seemingly nothing, memories that will be stirred within them for years to come: The tangy taste of homemade lemonade; the scratchiness of sand in their bathing suit; fireflies dotting the lawn; the smell of rain after a sun-shower, or the smoky smell of the barbeque.

"Slow down in our town." It's not just about driving a car. It's about driving your life and that of your child's.

In the lyrics of another long-ago summer ditty comes more truth:

"Slow down, you move too fast.
You got to make the morning last.
Just kicking down the cobble stones.
Looking for fun and feelin' groovy.

Got no deeds to do,
No promises to keep.
I'm dappled and drowsy and ready to sleep.
Let the morning time drop all its petals on me.
Life, I love you,
All is groovy."

7
THE MYSTICAL, MAGICAL, MUCH-MALIGNED MOM

Mom: Time to Take Care of You

"If it is woman's function to give, she must be replenished too," wrote Anne Morrow Lindbergh over 50 years ago in "Gift from the Sea," and although I cannot be anywhere nearly as eloquent, I will attempt to convince you—busy, giving mom—to allow yourself permission to be replenished.

One day about six years ago, as I went on and on with the litany of the responsibilities of my day, a very wise woman grabbed me by the shoulders and implored, "What are you doing for *Julie?*"

I thought for a millisecond and replied, "Does shopping at the Gap count?"

She practically glared at me. "No! If you don't take care of you, you won't be any good at taking care of everybody and everything else."

Mothers take care of children, of the carpooling, of the house, of the husband. Sometimes, as they and their own parents' age, they take care of their mom and dad, too. Life throws in other stresses and problems, some high class (renovating a house) and often more serious (divorce, illness, troubled teens). Throw in a part or full-time job and boom: Mommy burn-out.

When my friend pointed out that I wasn't really doing much just for me, or trying to make life a tad less martyrish (a word I just invented), I started to re-prioritize. At first I felt horribly guilty when I took time out for Julie or ignored my "to do" list. A nap before the kids got home? How decadent! Not making dinner? Bad mommy-wifey-poo. A massage once or twice a month? How extravagant! Delegating or asking for help? Unheard of. I am in control and I can do it all. Actually, oh no, I can't. And you can't either. Here are just a few ways that you might be able to lighten your load, recharge, refuel, reinvent.

Two words: "Take-Out"

The fall and the spring are especially challenging for parents with children's sports, dance, and/or other extracurricular activities. Many after school commitments end or even begin at the dinner hour. It's difficult to plan and cook in the comfort of your own home with the crazy schedules of pick-up and drop-off. Sure, you *can* do it (crock pot, stir-fry), but on some days, why bother?

Many markets, delis and catering outlets have prepared foods and dinners-to-go just begging for you to come pick them up, take them home to reheat, or, in the case of pizza or Chinese food, simply dig right in!

Mother: Pamper Thyself

Massages, manicures, facials, and candle-lit baths all sound like the stuff of the very wealthy. But, trust me; they are for any woman, anywhere, anytime.

Instead of buying yet another pair of shoes for yourself or that sweater that you feel you *must* have, take that $75 or so and get a massage. It's as simple as cutting back on the weekly or monthly grocery expense. In other words:

think spiritual instead of material. And massages aren't just pampering; they are also very good for your circulation, your muscles, ergo—your physical health—as well as your mental well-being.

I started getting monthly and often twice-monthly massages when I seriously injured my back. Now I let the massage therapist work her magic on my body and my mind. Later, I am always much calmer with my kids and my husband as a result. Even just the massage you receive when getting a manicure is refreshing and de-stressing.

"Women need solitude in order to find again the true sense of themselves," wrote Lindbergh.

As for the candle-lit baths: Do it! And all by yourself; no husbands allowed. Draw one after the kids finally get to sleep at night or even before they get home from school. I am dead serious. Try it once and see what a difference it makes to just stop the world in the middle of the day, soak in a warm, bubbly and heavily-scented tub, and allow a few minutes to think instead of do.

Delegate!

Do you really have to do it all? I don't think so. Ask for and accept help. Your driving-age teen can pick up your elementary-school-aged child at practice. Teach your 11-year-old the intricacies of the washing machine and dryer (my eight-year-old just taught *himself*! Thank you dear Jack!). When friends say, "What can I do to help?" let them do something, anything: take the kids after-school, pick-up your dry cleaning, visit your ailing parent, whatever.

While there are plenty of free ways to delegate, sometimes you have to pay a little bit for what amounts to a whole lot of help. I discovered a terrific new concierge service. Its owner is a godsend. She has done kid-sitting, of course, but has also driven to the hospital to pick up an MRI when I was out of town and needed it for an appointment upon my return. She's waited for the cable guy while I was unavailable to hang out all day, and has even picked up prescriptions for us when we were on a trip. This sort of service is becoming more and more popular around the country, and I recommend it when you are in a bind, or foresee one. Making life a little easier is the key for busy moms.

Remember: If the mommy ain't happy, ain't nobody happy!

Mothers and Daughters

Because my mother died recently, I have been doing a lot of thinking about mothers and daughters, and the all-too-often wonderfully complicated relationship that exists. "Complicated" doesn't necessarily connote anything negative; complicated is simply the word to use and it is truth of the matter where mothers and daughters are concerned.

I am blessed to have a daughter, Janet, nearly 12 years old. In a house sometimes overflowing with testosterone—three sons and a husband—Janet and I find sanctuary with one another. Now that she is getting older, we also share a love of shopping, of swapping shoes, the benefits of lip gloss, Emily Dickinson's poetry, and cranking hip-hop music with the car's sunroof open. On the flip side, as she dives head first into puberty and adolescence, we have both learned which buttons to push to elicit annoyance in the other, the drama of slamming bedroom doors and the "Good Lord" eye-roll.

I remember getting the results of the ultrasound which revealed that I was, in fact, carrying a girl. With two sons already, I was thrilled beyond thrilled that shades of pink would be invited into my life, along with frilly socks, cute headbands and sweet sundresses. It also meant I could look forward to—and currently engage in—discussions about boys and love, as well as soft kisses on my cheek forever.

My own mother and I had a complex relationship more in the negative vein, but it certainly wasn't without its joys. We would at once fear and revere the other, doubt the other's motives, become estranged, and then come close together again like giggly school girls. At her demise, we knew that love and respect had always been there.

"Why do you hate me?!" seems to be a not so uncommon wail from teenage daughters, at least according to those friends of mine who currently mother girls from ages 13 to 20. These women tell of seriously dramatic scenes and the parental consequences then set down (groundings, privileges revoked and the like). Just as with sons, these consequences are often necessary and aren't done in malice but rather, out of love. Teenaged boys may throw the phrase "why do you hate me?" out once or twice too, but it seems that girls use it as a mantra. Having been a teenager many moons ago, I remember that mantra well. The key for mothers is to keep reassuring the daughter (or son) that "hate" is not at all part of the equation. Sooner or later, the child will believe you, even if that child doesn't believe you until she is a parent herself.

As I grieve, I feel lucky now to have a daughter of my own. It actually makes the process a bit easier; I feel less alone. Janet's middle name is my mother's name, and like my mother, she has a great flair for the theatrical and a stubborn streak that is endearing in an oddly comforting way.

Girls aren't always easy to raise, but as my mom was fond of saying, "Easy isn't interesting." And so I rejoice in my daughter's accomplishments and hug her hard and find help when she stumbles. I adore waking up to find her snuggling next to me. She gives the best massages this side of a professional therapist and her dancing makes me laugh. It won't be—and hasn't been—all smooth sailing for us, but I will be always grateful that 12 years ago I was told, "It's a girl!"

Mothering Heights

When is a mother at her best? Is it at those moments of extreme pride and joy with her child? Or is it rather when her child is at their worst? I vote for the latter.

The height of motherhood is being able to love your child even when that child feels temporarily "unlovable." When the two-year-old tantrum takes on epic proportions; when pushes become shoves on the playground and your child is branded a bully; when your 11-year-old shouts at you like a whiny, drunken sailor on leave; or when the impulsivity of adolescence reaches a cringe-worthy, dodgy low.

The strength of motherly love is in our ability to distinguish between the "not-my-child" and the "oh-no-it—*is*-my-child" train of thought; of separating fact from fiction. Making your child aware of your disappointment or disillusionment with their actions, combined with your unconditional love in the face of the good, the bad and the ugly may be what the kid remembers most down the line: "You are not a disappointment; your actions are."

In their heart of hearts your child knows they tripped up modestly or spectacularly. Even more key is the fact that you know it, accept it. You mete out the appropriate consequences (if the school or law enforcement or who-knows-who hasn't beaten you to the punch). And you remind your child that you love him or her, and that you have the faith they can reach better decisions in the future.

If you can't surrender to the reality that your angel can or will temporarily morph—however briefly or long-term—into a demon child, then you and your offspring may have a decidedly difficult time moving on through life. Bad things happen to good people, and good people may occasionally perpetuate bad things. But if "bad" kids are made to feel like the victim of their victims by their parents, life lessons and morals are probably rarely learned. Tough love is often more potent than easy love.

Of course we mothers are universally known for that easy love as well.

The heights of my own easy love spring quickly to mind, even in the recent face of some trips and stumbles among my four grown and on-the-grow kids. Witness the bursting elation and physical leap I make and feel every time I greet Blake at Kennedy airport after a return from combat, or a simple long absence between leaves. The unbridled thrill I deployed the day of Kenny's college graduation when he surprised us with the news of being named valedictorian and commencement speaker. Watching Jack out on the baseball diamond as he hits and catches with confidence and success. The kick of observing the blinding bliss on Janet's face as she performs. They know I love them then, when actions are uncomplicated and tailor-made for a mother's strong hugs and misty eyes.

Being their mother, they know, is also to question their behaviors, their plans, their obvious-to-me dubious choices. I can guide, I can cajole, prod, poke, ground, deny and/or punish. As long as I do it with a healthy dose of love they will realize that as people they are anything but a disappointment.

And that I, too, will not have been a disappointment as their mother.

Every Day is Mother's Day

On one Mother's Day back in the early 1960's, my brother and I asked our mom why there was a "Mother's Day" holiday. She answered, "Because *every* day is 'Kids' Day.'" I recall us looking at one another with a mixture of guilt and glee. I also recall the guilt quickly fleeing. "*Kids'* Day? Cool!"

My own Mother's Days—and there have been 20 of them!—are pretty nice, but nothing extraordinary. I sleep late, maybe the kids bring me some breakfast in bed, I get both homemade and Hallmark-produced cards, and we go out for dinner or order my favorite take-out. Kind of like most Sundays, except for the cards!

There was one Mother's Day, however, that does stand out. When my now 19-year-old son Kenny, was 12, he spent about an hour in his room with the door locked, banging on the walls. I was trying to nap and it drove me crazy, but he wouldn't let me in. Finally he asked me to come to his bedroom. "Okay, just slowly open the door," he instructed, as the rest of the family stood outside with him in the hallway. As I turned the knob and began to walk in, my then-favorite song (R. Kelly's "I Believe I Can Fly") started playing. In the darkened room Christmas lights blinked brightly; lights that had been strung up all over one wall to read: "Mom." It was a very memorable and treasured moment.

Don't get me wrong, I do love the plaster handprints, the Popsicle frames and the tiny flowers grown in egg cartons. They are beyond special. I also adore the placemats with poems laminated onto them forever, as well as the wire hangar mobiles. But it's the everyday gifts that my children bring me that mean the most.

My daughter Janet and I will sometimes have a girl day on a random Saturday or Sunday. We'll get a manicure; see a movie, the obligatory after-movie ice cream, and an hour of window shopping or actual shopping. During which she will open up her little heart to me about all manner of subjects. I'm her confidant, and her temporary guide through the beginnings of middle school, and it is an honor. When she comes home with a passing grade in a subject she was struggling with, and thanks me for helping, that's a gift, too. An unexpected but needed hug from Janet when I've had an emotionally draining day on the war watch is the best present, too.

When Jack, eight, wants me to lie down next to him and cuddle at bedtime: great gift. The first time Kenny called from college this school year and solicited my advice and took it: awesome moment. The fact that he phones me after he leaves each final exam to tell me he's aced it: priceless. Blake emailing me from Fallujah last Friday: you can imagine how incredible.

Every day can be Mother's Day if you but look for the kudos your kids are giving you. They are there, sometimes buried, sometimes right between your eyes. Yet, it is still nice to have one day named after us mothers and to have your spouse shower you with praise and spring posies. And this year, honey, a spa gift certificate would be oh-so-lovely as well. Remember: Father's Day is *next* month. A gift other than a tie would be welcome, no?

The Difference between Loving Mommy and Missing Mommy

This is the summer that I have learned that my children always love me even if they don't always (if at all!) miss me.

My 19-year-old, Kenny, was coming home from college for one week starting on the Fourth of July weekend. His school goes year 'round (he will get his B.A. in two years as opposed to four). We had planned his flights months ago, but in the meantime, had decided that we would spend the weeks before and after the Fourth up at our family home on Martha's Vineyard.

"Certainly Kenny will join us," I determined.

"Certainly not!" thought Kenny.

Hanging out with boyhood friends, visiting his former boss and buddies at the pastry shop where he had worked senior year, and enjoying a briefly parentless home for a few days was his idea of paradise. Kicking back with mom on the Vineyard beaches was not an option.

"Okay, I'll see ya the night before I go back!" he chirped. "Love you, mom!"

No missing of the mother. No great need for my sandwich making skills or my spaghetti Bolognese. He was perfectly content with a brief evening of my charm and wit and a drive to the airport the next day, while I could have spent hours chatting and laughing and just hearing him lumber about the house.

This past year was my first with a half-empty nest. Although the younger two clearly fill my time, my head and my home with a lot of chatter and constant need, I really have missed Kenny and Blake. And it kind of stinks that the missing is just a one-way proposition.

Every letter or email that I have sent to Blake in Iraq ends with "I miss you." I haven't seen him since Thanksgiving '03; that is the longest I have gone without seeing him in nearly 21 years. Okay, okay, I know that this is what happens: the children grow and go and you don't see them that often. But this child is in a war, and we cannot speak to one another, and it is different.

A couple of months ago we were able to instant message for the first and only time.

Me—"Do u miss us?"

Blake—"Do u want the truth or should I tell u what u want to hear?"

Me—"What I want to hear although that's kind of crummy of u."

Blake—"I just don't miss things."

Me—"Don't u miss your Jeep? Home-cooked meals? Cookies? Ice cream? My smile …?"

Blake—"Maybe the Jeep a little." Ouch for the terrified, missing-her-son-like-crazy mommy.

Two weeks ago I received a letter from him with a bit more explanation: "Just because I don't miss you doesn't mean I don't love you. You need to understand that. Be strong; I'll take care of myself and get myself back home."

And so that is what happens. We give our children roots and wings, it has been said. Once they're off and flying there is still love, just not a whole lot of missing going on.

As my own parents were dropping me off at college, my father looked at me with tears in his eyes and cried, "Flap your wings, baby Julie! You're leaving the nest!" I hugged him and my mother, waved good-bye and didn't give them a second thought until I needed money and English literature advice.

What goes around comes around. In my teens and 20's I was full of love for my parents, but it wasn't until I, too, became a parent that I started to miss my own, and of course, appreciate them.

Janet, 11, leaves in a few days for a four-week ranch camp in Wyoming. Maybe *she'll* miss me a little. Maybe it's just a late teen thing when you still love, but don't miss your parents. Or maybe I will be three for four this summer.

Sigh. Guess both loving and missing is a parent's job. At least for now.

Worry Is a Mom's Middle Name

On the day that I write this, a U.S. Marine helicopter was shot down by insurgents in Iraq, killing 31 Marines from the First Marine Division, the same division with which my oldest son, Blake, is attached. Blessedly, Blake is not back in the sandbox at the moment, but rather training for Special Forces in California. Nevertheless, my heart still sunk at the news, and while grateful that my son is safe, I felt deeply saddened for the mothers of those Marines who were not so fortunate.

And I worry. I worry about Blake being sent back there—his former unit will be re-deployed next month—and I worry about the dangers inherent in his new line of work in defending and serving our country and our military. My friends worry for me and acquaintances worry, too; even strangers worry. Strangers who may have heard of Blake, but have never met him or me. Although the concern comes from both sexes, it is my fellow moms that seem to worry the most. (Fathers: Please note the use of the word "seem.")

Worrying is what moms do, and oh, we do it well, and with vigor. Whether it is something as frightening as a child in war or as common as a child flying too high on a swing, we worry. Worry forms in bold capital letters in our head and across our hearts from the moment our children are born: "I worry that he won't breast-feed;" "I worry that she cries too much;" "What if he's too cold in that onesie?" or "What if she's too warm?" Those worries grow in size and strength, as do our children.

How many times do we hear our children cry, "Don't worry so much, mom!" That's how it works—moms worry, kids get to whine about it and hopefully everything turns out okay, or if it doesn't, then lessons are learned, sometimes on both sides.

Jack played football for the first time last fall. Although he wore a lot of padding and a solid helmet, I worried about him getting hit too hard. Of course, getting hit was exactly what his father looked forward to. "It's fine, Jul," Jon assured me. "If Jack knows you're worried he may not want to hit and then he will get tackled hard. Getting knocked around a little never hurt anybody …" Oh sure, I thought, as I braced myself with every play, and thought briefly of knocking my *husband* around. But Jon was right, and my worrying, although not completely unfounded, was still not needed.

Often it is best not to wallow in the worry and just as often it is difficult not to. I have been told to "turn it over." I have had to attempt that and continue doing so with Blake. When Kenny was going through some adolescent fits and starts I was worried constantly, but eventually I began to adjust my worry level with him. With Janet I worry about middle school and its social and educational stresses. With Jack I worry about his frustration level and its impact on school and his buddies. My friends worry about their children off at boarding school or college, of the son who just got his driver's license, of the daughter struggling with eighth grade science, and the twins getting into a private school. The outcome of most of these worries is truly out of our control. The trick is differentiating which stuff is worth sweating over and which isn't.

I worry about terrorism, botulism, racism, alcoholism, pessimism. Should I be worried that my daughter will be kidnapped when walking from school to town? How worried should I be about Jack testing the frozen-ability of our shallow backyard pond? Will Kenny get a job after he graduates from college in May? Should I obsess about a Marine in dress blues ringing my doorbell one evening? The answers are both yes and no. If I didn't love my children so much, I wouldn't worry, and therein lies the rub.

Oddly enough, I have a saying posted on the bulletin board in my home office which reads: "Worrying does not empty tomorrow of its troubles; it empties today of its strength." There are days when I can look at that and say, "Yeah! How true! I can do that," and other days when I want to shred that saying to pieces. Yet I always hear my children—actually, primarily Blake—crying like a mantra in my head: "You worry too much mom. Everything's going to be okay. Calm down."

"*Hakuna Matata*," sang Timon and Pumba in the movie "The Lion King." According to the characters, it means: "No worries for the rest of your days." I think it's worth humming that song whenever the worry kicks in. Try it. If nothing else, it will make you giggle and forget your worries for a moment.

8
WHAT THE TEENS MEAN

Not So Idle Idol Worship

All four walls of my daughter's bedroom, and a good piece of her ceiling, are plastered with magazine photos of child actors Dylan and Cole Sprouse. She is obsessed—and by her own admission, addicted,—to these twin stars of the Disney channel series, "The Suite Life of Zack and Cody." The rest of our family is amused at the extent of the idol worship.

At age 13, I too was pretty obsessed with the 1960's televised singing group, The Monkees, and adorable member Davy Jones in particular. My room was a shrine of self-designed Davy collages from *Teen Beat* magazine and its ilk. Davy was five feet, four inches tall, and when I reached that same height at the end of seventh grade, I squealed; me and Davy! Height-mates as well as soul mates!

Most children experience a celebrity crush or fascination at some point. It's a rite of passage. Admiring those in the limelight isn't unhealthy, unless of course, one becomes a stalker, of which I sometimes believe Janet may be capable.

Blake really enjoyed Michael Jackson's music for a few years back in the late 1980's, until he learned that Wacko-Jacko was in truth African-American and not Caucasian. It was the weirdness factor, not prejudice, which made him shudder thereafter whenever Michael's songs came on the car radio. Blake later went on to greatly admire basketball great Larry Bird, whom he slightly resembled during high school.

Kenny, too, became fixated on a basketball legend: Magic Johnson. The interesting aspect of this, was that it was during Magic's infamous press conference regarding his HIV diagnosis and retirement, that then seven-year-old Kenny decided to begin collecting all things Magic. His bedroom walls and shelves were transformed into a shrine to Johnson. He possessed the Laker's jersey emblazoned with his hero's number 32, and I even found him a large, stuffed Magic Johnson doll. He was thrilled beyond thrilled when one day the autographed photo of Johnson he so desired arrived in the mail. In addition, the Polaroid of Kenny himself in full #32 regalia was thoughtfully returned with Magic's signature across the photo.

Kenny, Blake and I never met the objects of our desire, but Janet was recently able to meet hers. (She has been telling me that it was her life's goal to meet these twins; I'm so proud that this and not discovering a cure for cancer, or helping undernourished children was her aspiration. Cue my rolling eyes).

Earlier this month, upon discovering that the boys were to be at Manhattan's Planet Hollywood for a launch party of their new magazine, *Code*, I took Janet, her friend Bria, and younger brother Jack into the city. After standing behind velvet ropes protecting a pretty ratty looking red carpet for a couple of hours, the boys arrived to high pitched screams from the other dozens of pre-and early teenaged girls. As Cole made his way down our side of the ropes, Janet stood frozen and shaking as Cole approached her and Bria. At least Bria had the presence of mind to acquire an autograph. As Cole and Dylan ducked into the restaurant, Janet's shaking became more pronounced as she alternately cried and smiled. Suddenly, she dashed in after them, with the three of us scrambling to catch her. As the twins signed autographs on the fourth floor of the restaurant, the kids watched through the glass walls on the third floor, snapping pictures of these mini-heartthrobs from their cell phones.

Later, on the train ride home, it looked as though Janet was floating on air. She positively glowed. She had been *thisclose* to her idols. I asked if she was happy.

"Yes, but I didn't get to talk to them," she frowned slightly and added, like a true addict, "That's my next goal." If one time is good, then another is better. More is lovely. So, now it's a conversation. And the small matter of a marriage proposal from Dylan Sprouse.

My Davy Jones era ended nearly as quickly as it had begun, but I don't think the Sprouse twins will disappear from her radar any time soon. Nevertheless, I find myself hoping that she'll instead develop a wild, *requited* crush on an eighth grade boy next year which will eclipse the Dylan fixation.

Once upon a time, your parents are the heroes, and then inexplicably, we are relegated to the realm of the dispensable. But I don't full-heartedly truly believe that. We parents rock, even if it takes decades for our kids to shine up our tarnished crowns.

Surviving Sleepovers

Ah, the sleepover.

Marriage, of course, constitutes the ultimate sleepover; hopefully, one gets to spend every night of one's life with the same best buddy. And, often with marriage comes parenthood, and then one is afforded the opportunity to truly experience the joys and jungle warfare of one's child's sleepover.

I titled this "surviving," not to indicate that all sleepovers are horrible, terrible, very-bad things, because they most certainly are not (yet some are undeniably not the most restful of events). Nor does the title imply that I posses any clever tips. I merely have anecdotes, and maybe there is an "Ah-Ha!" moment in one of these for you, the newbie—or not-so-newbie—parent of a sleepover-aged child.

To my mind, the definition of a "sleepover" is your child having one friend to spend the night; more than one and it's a "slumber party" (girls only) or a "massacre" (boys only).

Blake was not big on having friends over to spend the night, and that was probably because one of his first sleepovers was such a nightmare for Jon and me. He was nine, and the buddy he invited was loud and rowdy. He egged Blake on to take all the posters off of his little brother's bedroom wall (Kenny was gone for the night at another's home) as well as pull the blankets and sheets off Kenny's bed. When we caught them in the act, Blake was immediately contrite, while his friend simply smirked. And after we announced "lights out," this boy kept on talking, laughing and shouting for at least another hour or two. In the morning—the wee hours of the morning, I might add—he was again talking loudly in the kitchen and turning the volume up on the television, even after we requested of Blake that it be turned down low. That was the very first and almost last time that a friend ever slept over. (In fairness, I need to report that that 10-year-old terror turned into a lovely young man, and Kenny, in fact, is roommates in New York City with him; his bedroom now goes untouched).

Kenny was and is more social than Blake, and so there were more sleepovers in his childhood, some of which were manageable on our nerves and some, alas, which were memorable in their destructiveness on our home and our amount of sleep. Boys will be boys will be boys, of course, but it was amazing how rude and/or disrespectful some of these little men could be in our home.

And then, of course, there were the gems, the sincerely sweet and nice, most notably a best friend of Ken's named Joe, who for several years became a fixture in our house every weekend until the boys reached about age 14 or 15.

Because of the older two children, we have learned with Janet and Jack to state the ground rules for having a friend spend the night: stop running about like mad monkeys when we ask. Don't do something you know we won't like, even if your friend encourages you otherwise, and keep it down in the morning.

However, having a daughter means hosting bona fide slumber parties. "Slumber party" is such an oxymoron. "Slumber" is so very much not part of the equation for the guests as well as the parents. As a preteen, I adored slumber parties. As a parent, I always wonder two hours into them why I agreed to such a giggle and high-pitched scream-fest. Yes, of course I remember being 11, 12, 13 and 14, with boys on the telephone and sugar and salty treats up the wahzoo, plus loud music and unbridled hilarity. I also now know why the slumber party-hosting mothers and fathers of my friends always looked so unkempt, sleepy, and seemed just ever so slightly on edge the morning after a giant sleepover. And I apologize, belatedly, to them all!

Spending the night with a friend is a right of passage for all children, paving the way for good or bad roommate behavior down the line. All I can say in closing, fellow parents, is that what goes around comes around, and goes around again. Be prepared to offer solace in the future when your then-grown son or daughter calls you after their child's first sleepover, and try and resist the "payback's a …" comment.

The Lowdown on Crushes

School's well underway and there are new boys or girls in your child's class, or members of their grade who heretofore were invisible. Yet somewhere between June and September they emerged from their ugly duckling stage and will be whispered about in small groups as looking "so hot."

I cringe when I hear the adjective "hot" come out of a 12 or 13-year-old's mouth to portray another 12 or 13-year-old. I don't remember hearing that depiction of a handsome boy or a beautiful girl until somewhere in my 20's, yet even then the word was mostly employed when speaking about porn stars. Yeah, yeah, it's a new millennium and all of that. But really—that description of another coming from a middle or high schooler's mouth?!

Adolescent crushes will begin forming, people, as sure as yellow buses appearing 'round the bend and new textbooks cracking open. You may even overhear your sweet little daughter referred to as "hot" while passing a pod of boys downtown after school. The crushes will last for days or weeks, or maybe just until gym class. Your son or daughter will blush or stammer or stutter, and shyly tell you about the cute person, hoping for your discretion.

I recall Blake and Kenny's first crushes with fondness, even though they remember my reaction quite differently. Kenny's was with an adorable girl who was in his third grade class; her name was Stacey. She was a tiny and perky ballet dancer, with long brownish-blond hair who would giggle whenever she was near Kenny. He would alternate between ignoring her and chasing her around the playground trying to kiss her.

Because I was then publishing *County Kids*, I thought it would be nice to put her on the cover for our annual dance issue. Wouldn't Kenny be thrilled? He could frame the cover and pine over her in the privacy of his own home. When her mother accepted the offer, I was pleased and Kenny was perplexed. To him, it seemed a public admission of his crush. No sooner had the issue hit the stands than he announced that he "hated" her. I had crushed the crush and he's never let me forget it.

"Don't ever do to Janet and Jack what you did to me with Stacey!" he screamed at me at age 15 a propos of nothing. Blake echoed his brother's thoughts, as one year after the Stacy incident I had put Blake, his buddy and the object of his affection on the cover of *County Kids*. Needless to say, neither son confides in me the existence of a romantic relationship lest I now start planning a wedding and imagining what my grandchild might look like.

Crushes are fun (although unrequited ones aren't as gleeful), they're innocent and they produce the kind of butterflies that make one's heart soar. Even adults can develop crushes. I have a number of female friends who have admitted harmless crushes on tennis instructors, or the cute father they see in the school hallway, or on the football field, or the handsome police officer. Even my male friends will cop to the occasional attraction towards the adorable wife of a friend of theirs. As long as the crushes don't progress to something more adulterous, it seems okay.

Your child's object of fascination may reciprocate the affection and become a boyfriend or girlfriend which is another rite of passage entirely. (Don't worry neophytes of this phenomenon, all it means is that they instant message one another and perhaps hang out on Friday afternoons.)

So gear up. Along with fresh pens and pencils, your child may acquire the preteen or teenage crush. It's your job not to squash their foray into "love." Today's hot crush is tomorrow's in-law.

I may not like the word "hot," but no matter what you call it, crushes are cool. Until the next time.

Preteens in Connecticut

School is in session (I see you smiling at that), and among other things, it means that this afternoon there will be a swarm of preteens making their way into town.

They will be humming outside the candy store. Small pods of preteens will snake Main Street, visiting Starbucks and Baskin Robbins. And duos of girls will attack CVS in search of the perfect lip gloss. (Yes, by fifth grade this is an obsession; don't fight it. Just guard your own!) Your younger children will stare and covet these middle schoolers' independence. Your older children may sneer—being above all that now—or they may grin in silent remembrance.

If you are a parent of a 10 to 12-year-old, you will be neither smiling, nor sneering. Most likely, you will be sighing quite heavily, shaking your head ever so slightly, curiosity swirling in your stomach, and wondering what happened to your baby boy or girl.

As a survivor of two teenage-hoods, I can tell you that the years between 11 and 18 are truly a test for both parent and child. There will be tears. There will be fears. There will be hugs and there will be slammed doors. There is a pulling away, and then a staying put.

One son made it through those seven years with little incidence; the other put us through a test to end all tests of character, strength and patience, and ever-so-briefly, a test of love. Now 19, he is a sweet, well-adjusted, responsible young man. Seven years later, I am older and wiser.

So, my preteen, Janet, had better watch out! I'm pretty sure that I have been through the wringer and I am now better prepared for what her next several years bring to her and to us.

While hiking down a mountain last week, Janet began singing a song she had written, and during the next seven miles of our journey, she finished it. It's called "Preteen in Connecticut," and I want to share it with you—parents of children of all ages—as the lyrics seemed to me to truly describe what goes on during those years where hormones begin to trickle and the yearning for self-expression builds.

Preteen in Connecticut

I may be young, but I don't care

I've got some talent that you can't bear.

Most people like me, but you can choose

Make the right decision; don't lose.

I love my friends and my "fam,"

If people talk about me I don't give a d_ _ _.

I'm just a pre-teen in Connecticut

And nothing that I do is going to be perfect.

I keep on growing every day

And I keep changing in every way.

I live my life the way I want to,

Not the way that people tell me to.

I've climbed a mountain and I've roped a calf

And I'm well-known to make people laugh.

Yeah, I'm funny, but that's not all.

Don't you dare call me small.

I've got three brothers that made me tough

And now I know that I'm good enough.

I'm just a preteen in Connecticut

And nothing that I do is going to be perfect.

I keep on growing every day

And I keep on changing in every way.

The Wonder Years, Mean Tweens and Self Image

"Wow, what a day! Bob probably hates me. Tenley and I called Marc and got into a big fight. And Marc called Bob and … Ooooh! I really goof up everything!" This was an entry from my sixth grade diary in 1968. It was a typical entry, a snippet of my reality at ages 11 through 13; the thick of the wonder years.

My feelings and emotions were as ferocious as they were fickle. One week after the above entry, I was smitten by a dark-haired boy named Kevin. I also hated my hair, thought myself to be ugly, but was still sure that I was "kinda popular." I do not miss those days of running hot, then cold.

Just how full of wonder are the middle school years in 2004? The years between ages 10 and 14 are incredibly different that they were in the 1960's. Life—family life alone—is much more diverse. And yet, the whole scenario of the old television program "The Wonder Years" is the same today as it was 40 years ago: friendships, clothes and social status reign supreme. As a former middle school principal once said to me, "This is such a social age. Most kids would like to forget academics."

From my perspective, that seems to be true. I endured my two sons' middle school years and their not-so-stellar academic performances, and am now finishing up my daughter Janet's first year as a middle schooler. The boys were one thing, but my girl's antics are a whole different ballgame.

First there is the obsession with what clothes to wear and how she styles her hair. "You're just 11," I cry. "Grab a pair of pants and a shirt, brush your hair and boom! You're done." But no, so-and-so has made fun of the pants she was in love with last week and the t-shirt she swore she couldn't live without is today deemed "dorky." And she echoes her mommy as a girl when she wails, "I hate my hair!"

Next are the mean and hurtful things girls can say to one another, when most of the time they don't realize just how nasty they are actually speaking. One friend might accuse another of doing something hateful and the war of words that ensues sting deep and strong. Often with girls there is something altogether else going on, and some timely intervention can lead to both girls working out their misplaced anger.

I had my own brief flirtation as a mean tween back in sixth grade, when I found myself hurt and confused over a best friend's alliance with the "new girl." The girl in question was pretty and had the most amazing assortment of fish-net stockings. My friends and I were immediately jealous and suspicious. And so I spearheaded the "Alison Smith Hating Club." I even had the bad form to ask Alison to join!

"But I *am* Alison," she told me. I smiled back. "Yes, I know." Ouch!

The happy ending is that the club was quickly disbanded and Alison and I became fast and best friends throughout high school and beyond.

As I glance through my diaries, I try to remember and struggle to get a better handle on some of the ups and downs of those years when kids straddle the chasm between childhood and young adult.

Diary entry dated February 7, 1970 (Eighth grade): *"The semi-formal! My hair was all 'gooied' up and I wore my black velvet and satin outfit. David looked terrific. Stupid Robby didn't go. Poor Tenley. God! That Robby! Oh gosh—my math homework! Must go do it. See ya same time tomorrow, Diary!"*

Perhaps the more things change, the more they stay the same.

Alcohol Use: Facts, Feelings and Family

One evening 13 years ago, Jon, Kenny, Blake and I sat down for a celebratory dinner. I had just found out that I was pregnant (with Janet). We toasted— the boys with their milks and Jon and me with a glass of beer. Blake, then nine, stopped us mid-toast and cried, "Mommy! You can't drink beer when you're pregnant! Stop it!"

"You're right, Blake," I replied sheepishly, and I put my glass down, pushing it to the center of the table. Kenny, then seven, quickly picked it up, and before we knew it he had taken a big sip.

"Ahhh," he said, setting down the glass. "When I grow up I want to be a drunk!"

We all laughed a horrified laugh, but nobody was more horrified than me, who—at that point—was steeped deep in denial that I might actually be a "drunk," an alcoholic. Coming from a childhood where one of my parents was an alcoholic, I certainly didn't want one of my children becoming one.

Fact: Children of drinking parents are less likely to see drinking as harmful, and are more likely to start drinking earlier.

Fact: Alcohol is the number one drug of choice among our nation's youth.

These facts, from the Substance Abuse and Mental Health Services Administration, have been facts long before they were seriously looked into and surveys were taken. But that doesn't lessen the truth. And the truth is that a good number of students of middle and high school age experiment with and/or use alcohol. Some of their parents know it and many haven't a clue.

I am like white on rice with my kids about alcohol use and abuse. I easily and instinctively discovered Kenny's hiding places for booze back in high school, and lectured him and Blake about drinking and driving. Janet is in sixth grade and I weekly remind her that she shouldn't smoke a cigarette or drink alcohol just because a friend might offer either one. I am hyper vigilant because I am a recovering alcoholic and of course do not want to see any of my children tailspin into abuse and dependency on alcohol.

Does that fact mean that my children might be spared? Of course not. Will a non-alcoholic parent be spared a child using alcohol or drugs? Of course not as well.

Parents can exert a moderating influence on the drinking behavior of their adolescent children by monitoring their own alcohol use and that, too, is a studied fact. It might also be helpful to reach back into the memory of your own drinking or drugging history from high school in the 70's or '80's and use that knowledge to be aware of where your child might be hiding the evidence, or where he or she might choose to use right there in your own home.

Feeling: This knowledge may or may not prevent my younger children from taking a drink or two in the woods, at a friend's home with absent parents, or in a bathroom stall at school.

Fact: We are luckier than our own parents were because we are armed with the facts. And we should charge ourselves with acting upon those statistics regarding teens and drinking and make sure that we equip our offspring with consequences.

I have heard it is best not to engage a drunken child (or adult) with those punishments, those consequences, when they are in an inebriated state. Save it for morning when the natural consequences of drinking are raging around in their head and their body and remorse is more easily available. I certainly wish that had been so for me back in high school. As it was, neither parent made a peep, and it is only by grace that I am still here to tell the story.

Spring fever is in the air. Remember how that felt when you were a teenager, and try not to be too smug if you didn't use or abuse alcohol; your child isn't you. And knowledge is power.

9
FOCUS ON FATHERS

Daddies, Daddies Everywhere!

It's raining men.

Now that spring has sprung, it seems to me that there are dads sprouting up like so many perennials. They're on the various and varied playing fields coaching or cheering; they're decked out in spandex on their bicycles maneuvering the main streets and the back roads; they're jogging or walking or jauntily pushing toddlers in strollers, and they're showing up in town earlier in the weekday evenings, walking smartly with take-out cartons or Baskin Robbins treats.

It's spring fever with an eye on shortened workdays on summer Fridays. With lacrosse and baseball games starting at 5:30 or so, the daddies are cutting out of the city or the various corporate headquarters here in the state, and making a full-on effort to take in their son or daughter's athletic pursuit. And for a lot of us mommies, it's a welcome respite from being the sole mode of transportation to this, that and the other activity.

Last Tuesday evening, as I took in Jack's baseball game, my theory about dads didn't wholly pan out. My husband, Jon, had a meeting and when I asked my friend Jennifer Forese as to the whereabouts of her husband Jamie, he was also attending to a business dinner. Jennifer's taxi schedule for her four sons, however, illustrates my above point brilliantly.

On most weekday afternoons, Jennifer picks up her sons at two separate private schools. Then, it's back to the house for homework and a quick change into lacrosse or baseball gear, and a dash to practice or games. Last Tuesday, Jennifer arrived at Bobby's game having previously been watching older son, Jack, in lacrosse, bringing along another son, Mark, for a baseball game that would commence once our 10-year-olds were done with the diamond.

On Saturday afternoon and again on Sunday night, it was all dad Jamie's show.

"I do make more of an effort in the spring," said Jamie, during a Saturday baseball game. "Sometimes I need about two weeks in advance to clear my schedule for a Tuesday or Wednesday game, but it happens." As we spoke, his cell phone rang and he was running for his car to go fetch his son Jack from a friend's. Then he had to bring him home and quickly head back across town to finish watching Bobby's team emerge victorious. As he ran off to his car, though, I did giggle inside; something satisfying about seeing a dad behave more like a mom.

There are daddies everywhere during the other three seasons, of course, but—to me—the sightings are primarily on the weekends. Now I see dads out in the garden, or showing a son how to mow the lawn. I have noticed more fathers driving kids to school in the morning and dropping their offspring at soccer practice. Dads in suits are picking up daughters in tutus. I've even noticed a father or two during the week toting an infant under one arm while dashing into the market for a quart of milk and bread. It's nice. And I am sure the children appreciate seeing more of their fathers during the daylight hours.

I know that I enjoy it when Jon can get home earlier to fire up the barbeque, and throw Jack a few pitches or shoot some hoops. When Janet was a bit younger, she too would brighten when it was going to be daddy picking her up from a practice or a dance class on a Wednesday. Now, well

… she's nearly 13 and it seemingly doesn't matter much if Jon or I are around at all—unless she needs something at CVS, and then I'm thrilled to pass that drive off to Jon.

Yep, it's raining men alright. Daddy-men. Just like daffodils and tulips, it's always a sweet surprise in spring to see where in the town's landscape they'll pop up.

Giving Fathers Their Due

Since Father's Day is next weekend, I thought it best to write a bit about those not-so-few, those not-too-proud-to-admit-they're-great, dads.

One of my favorite great dad stories about my husband, Jon, dates back to the day he became a biological father. One year earlier he had become a step dad to Kenny and Blake, then seven and nine, respectively. But on May 21, 1993, he saw the birth of his own flesh-and-blood in little miss Janet. But, here's the incredible part: May 21, 1993 was also Kenny's eighth birthday! (Janet was a planned Cesarean section baby and for some reason 12 years ago, I thought it would be cute to give Kenny a baby sister for his birthday.)

Prior to choosing May 21st as the birth date, we had already planned a big party for Kenny at a Discovery Zone (think humongous ball pool). Rather than change that date—Lord forbid I reschedule the C-section!—we kept it as planned. And so, on that Friday morning at 8:24 a.m., Jon was present as his daughter was born. For the remainder of the day, until around 3 p.m., he took care of her as I lay useless in a hospital bed on a major morphine buzz.

At three o'clock., he dashed from the hospital back to where we were living at the time, met the boys off the school bus and went over to the Discovery Zone for two hours of cake and chaos with a dozen little boys. When the party was finished, he drove his step sons back to the hospital, so that they could meet their new baby sister.

Blake and Kenny entered the hospital room with frosting-encrusted hair (Jon revealed that there had been a cake throwing episode), and Jon looked exhausted, but still on that first-time-parent high. It was a great dad moment; a great dad day.

There are, of course, more nice anecdotes about the dad in our house—coaching a myriad of sports, attending orchestra and choral concerts, pitching in when I am unable. Some not-so-good stories could be told as well, but I want to keep this upbeat.

However, on that note, I believe more fathers would benefit by reading magazine articles or quick-read books regarding some of the child rearing topics du jour—bullying, internet safety, body image and girls, drug abuse, or even attending an evening or Saturday morning seminar. This is just a suggestion/observation, so that when a father returns from a stressful day or jam-packed business trip and his children seem to implode or explode on him, he'll have a better understanding of the *why* and be equipped with the *how*. It seems these days that both parents need to have an arsenal of knowledge on the care and feeding of the new millennium child.

But back to the good stuff. Dads really do get to have a lot of fun with their children. Dads buy the professional sports team tickets and gear their kid up at the souvenir stand after the game. Dads seem to make a camping trip not only sound like a cool adventure, but then make it so. Dads ignore the bedtime curfew more than moms, and kid especially love that. There are a lot of dads (like my husband) whose only culinary specialty is eggs or pasta, which also means more take-out or fast-food trips when mom is out or away for a few days. Dads, diners, donuts and Home Depot go together nicely.

I miss my own dad, who used to take my younger brother and me to different diners on Sunday mornings. We would explore hardware stores; fly kites at the beach; learn to race slot cars, and play pool in the bellies of bowling alleys up and down Route 1. My father was my biggest supporter, and I sorely long for that encouragement at times.

A father can gift his child with confidence if he so chooses. He can bestow not only fun, but discipline, games and strategies, courage and dreams. I hope that all fathers are rewarded this Father's Day with an unforgettable tie—the tie between father and child.

10
ASSESSING THE POTENTIAL BRAT

The Entitled Child

Here is a scary question: Are you raising an entitled child?

No parent sets out to raise a child that feels any or all material possessions should naturally come their way. Ideally, it would be best if our kids understood that things need to be earned or deserved based on merit, and that it is better to give than to receive. There are children half a continent away, or on the other side of the world, who have nothing or who have lost everything. To my children, I say: "Get out there and help raise money or clothes or books for them!"

Although I am not an expert, I do have one frightening tale of an entitlement-minded child to share. When my second oldest son, Kenny, was an early teen, his favorite mantra was that he needed (fill-in-the-blank) because it was "pivotal to my success." The first time he said this I laughed and promptly went out and bought him whatever small piece of technology he had requested. And then it happened a second and a third time; I was becoming brainwashed to the phrase "pivotal to my success." Because I wanted him to be a success I robotically dashed to the store, whipped out the checkbook or the credit card and got him what he wanted. If he asked to stay up a little later at night, or have a friend sleep over, or drink Capris Suns until the cows came home—boom! His wish was my command. It was "pivotal to his success" and I felt I had to help make that happen. It was pivotal to my success as a parent. Oh, was I so very wrong, and Kenny and I both paid the price at times.

Flash forward to his senior year in high school. He went out and got a job at a pastry shop to pay for anything that might be a *want* rather than a *need*. In spite of feeling that he was entitled to us paying for college, he secured student loans (If he messed up in college it would be on his dime, not ours). The results? He graduated valedictorian last spring and anything that is still pivotal to his success is primarily bought by money he has earned. He has become entrepreneurial rather than entitled, a solid citizen rather than a self-seeking one.

Just because we can afford to buy X, Y, or Z for our kids doesn't mean we are going to buy it. We are trying to encourage our daughter to think beyond her own needs—"$60 jeans? *Really?*"—to those of others, known and unknown to her or our family. That just because it's the weekend doesn't mean she can stay up until midnight, or that her younger brother can continue not to eat what the rest of the family is eating just because he doesn't like the food.

The only two people entitled to do anything are mom and dad—we are entitled to try and raise children who have some sense of dollars and cents and right and wrong.

Instantly Gratified Kids

"Good things come to those who wait," is a concept that seems to fly right over the current generation's head. The "I-want-what-I-want-and-I-want-it-now" train of thought no longer seems to pertain to addicts. It can also apply to the tiny and not-so-tiny pod of children growing up in today's world. They are addicted to *now*.

With a bastion of micro-waveable treats, instant music via I-tunes; cell phones; movies-on-demand (apt moniker); Amazon.com overnight delivery; digital and cell-phone cameras allowing immediate glossy photos in hand or to the eye, and a myriad of additional conveniences and electronics of the 21st century, getting on-the-spot satisfaction is easy.

As I was mulling over this column's theme, my daughter unwittingly illustrated the topic perfectly. She asked me to blow-dry her hair (because doing it herself would be too timely and too much work?). As she complained about how long it was taking (are you *kidding* me?!), I offered sarcastically that perhaps someone could create a dryer that zaps the hair dry and straight in under 30 seconds. "Oh!" she exclaimed excitedly, "that would be soooo cool! Awesome! Do you think someone will invent that?"

"Probably," I muttered under my breath, eyes rolling in my head. Whatever happened to waiting, to going to a store to buy an album/CD; to needing to get *home* before calling a friend?

Here is a sampling of the requests and statements in our household: "Can we go to the video store now? I want the Star Wars video game;" "Just order take-out, mom. It takes too long for you to cook;" and "I don't want to do temp jobs. My website will make a million immediately." Or this one: "I need new jeans. Can you go get some while I'm in school?" Last time I checked I was a parent, not a manservant. Or are they one and the same now and I have I enabled myself to act as such?

I recall almost with fondness how my friends and I needed to wait to save our allowance to go to the nearby department store to buy an album in the record department, or purchase some hoop earrings from our favorite clothing store. Once the money was saved we had to bide our time a bit longer until one of our parents was available able to drop us off downtown. Getting pictures from homecoming took about a week to be developed. Fast food meant a peanut butter and jelly sandwich.

It's not only the kids who are used to instant gratification; we adults have hopped on the magic carpet ride to immediacy. Because it's available. With a click of the mouse we can avoid driving to the shoe store and instead find a pair of shoes boxed and on our doorstep within 24 hours. Netflix provides movies in the mail instead of searching for a parking space in town. I can log on to the computer at any time of day or night and search out what's going on in Iraq, or read a quick email from Blake, rather than wait an interminable amount of time as did my military family predecessors during World War 2 and Vietnam. An email "thank you" replaces the lost art of letter writing.

Even though the tools and technologies of without-delay exist in our world, maybe we can still take the time (all puns intended) to model delayed gratification and engage in some old-fashioned methods to retrieve and acquire an object of desire or necessity. Drive into town to rent a movie. Once in a while disallow cell phones and laptops on vacation (come on; you can do it Mr. or Mrs. Busy-pants). Let your pre-driving teen cool her heels for half an hour when she calls and proclaims that you pick her up *now*. There's no need for you to drop what you were doing unless it's an emergency. Diet pills, starving and incessant exercise, and/or liposuction to attain a rail-thin body isn't nearly as healthy as simply eating smaller meals, and running a few miles a week to teach our daughters that skinny doesn't equal self-esteem. Blue jean, sneakers or video game buying can wait until the weekend.

In a nutshell, we can teach this: Gratification can be achieved the old-fashioned way—by earning it.

11
PARENTING POINTERS TO PONDER

Do I Slow Down Enough for my Kids?

Last Sunday, I woke up with a long list of things that I needed to do and deadlines I had to meet. My husband had gone into the office and my mind was working overtime as to how I could fit in all my plans and not neglect Jack and Janet since I was the only parent on call. My needs were winning out in my mind. But, as I came dashing down the stairs in search of morning caffeine, Jack called out from the den asking me to see what he was watching on the television. My knee-jerk reaction was, "Just a minute! I need to do something first!" And then I heard him sigh and groan sadly and loudly. I padded toward him instead of the kitchen.

He was watching "Home Alone," every nine-year-old boy's fantasy. I sunk onto the couch next to him and quickly recalled that years ago I had taken Blake and Kenny, now 22 and 20, to see this movie when they were around Jack's age. Offering me part of the fleece throw, Jack snuggled close and we gasped and giggled for the next half an hour until I realized that I really did have to get a shot of caffeine. All that Jack needed to begin his day was a shot of my time.

There are moments of our children's lives that even the best intentioned of parents miss. Those first steps, first words, school parties or parades, athletic games, dance recitals. I was a full-time working mother with all four of the kids up until 1999, and wasn't available to participate in or at many events. Yet, even when I was available, I wasn't always "available;" my needs and wants would sometimes—can sometimes—come fast and furious.

"In a minute, honey!" "Later! I'm busy right now!" "I can't, sweetie. I have to go out." "I'll help you when I'm done with (fill-in-the-blank)." If you as a parent can't identify with one or more of these phrases, I would love to hear from you.

When our children are newborns, infants and toddlers, we can't afford to mutter the above. The kids are tiny or helpless, too dependent upon full parental attention and affection. As they become older and more self-sufficient it is easier to defer to "later." But what if later never comes?

There are certain topics, emotions and feelings that I wish I had spoken of and shared, with my own parents. I never said a final goodbye and "I love you" to my father nine years ago just before he died. I had warning, I had time. But when my mother phoned from Virginia to tell me he had but days left, I was in the middle of production for *County Kids* magazine and couldn't possibly see how I—the owner and publisher—could leave right away. He passed away the morning that I finally left Connecticut. That career blinders-on mentality, the "later" in reverse cost me dearly. I did not repeat that mistake nine months ago when my mother died.

My last Sunday morning scenario had interestingly also played out earlier this past week with Kenny, the 20-year-old. He was to move into New York City on the weekend and was packing up his stuff. I was doing my usual morning headless chicken routine, flashed him a morning smile, and flew out the door to a meeting. Upon my return an hour later, he was sitting in the den, also watching an old movie: "One Flew over the Cuckoo's Nest." My mind was racing with the to-do list engraved in my head, yet I nevertheless found myself slipping onto the couch next to Ken. It was an unconscious/conscious move.

He hadn't asked me to watch with him, but his smile and the conversation afterward suggested that he was very pleased that I had done just that, and I found that I didn't regret a moment I had spent with and on my older boy. The other stuff was and is just details—busy-making as opposed to memory-making.

Being five minutes late to work or a meeting, a luncheon, a dinner; grocery shopping later rather than sooner; checking our email or snail-mail after answering our child's query first; watching a good or even god-awful television show with our son instead of running to pay bills, or going for a run, or even running a company—these are the moments we will not regret. Regrets are natural. But they don't have to be frequent.

Encouraging your Child's Dreams

"Find something he's passionate about," I was advised during my son Kenny's turbulent, self-imploding adolescence. "He needs something to feel good about; something that's his own." He found it all by himself: Music. It got him through the end of those uneasy teenage years; he excelled in recording arts in college, and as an almost 22-year-old seems to be on the brink of great success.

Encouraging your child's—your teen's—passions may just spare him/her some potentially devastating forays into plunging self-esteem and the self-harm that often comes along with that territory (substance abuse, suicidal ideation, eating disorders and on and on). It's human nature to want to feel good and confident in oneself and one's abilities. A little praise about a passion can go a long way.

Growing up, I often felt not good enough, not thin enough, smart enough, popular enough, and so on. In hindsight and with age and maturity, I know that I was, of course, *more* than enough. My parents encouraged my ability to put more than two words together in a creative or inspiring way. I hung on to that praise. Yet, after questioning my desire to make a living one day as a writer ("I'm not good enough"), I sought advice from my sophomore English teacher. "A writer writes," said my sage instructor simply. "You're a writer. So write."

With four children ranging in age from 11 to 23, I hope that I have encouraged their abilities and their dreams. It's still—they are still—a work in progress.

Jack is a good athlete. Like a lot of young boys, he has announced that he wants to be a professional ball player, specifically, a baseball player. For the New York Yankees. Is that his destiny? Who knows? But championing his love of sports can at the very least make him turn out to be a team player in whatever career he ultimately winds up with as an adult. An athlete "athletes?" A player plays.

We're still waiting for more cues from Janet. She seems to really enjoy the performing arts and states that she wants to be an actress one day. I'm not sure I see that fire-in-the-belly needed to pursue such a calling, but that may just materialize with time and experience. She is passionate and a bit obsessed with a certain set of twin television/film actors, and if we can just turn that desire away from them and instead onto her own possible thespian strengths, things may head in a different direction. An actress acts.

Blake, the oldest, showed great aptitude towards drawing and sketching as a child and teenager. We applauded his flair with art lessons, tools of the trade and talk of art college. At the same time, he was fascinated with the military. Blake was the child who always dressed as a soldier for Halloween, enjoyed watching retrospectives of various wars on the History Channel, loved hunting with his father, and announced to me during his sophomore year that he wanted to be a Navy SEAL or a Marine.

"What about art?" I asked nervously. "You're so talented!"

The next thing I knew, I was buying him books on the SEALS, videos of the Marine Corps, and camouflage tee-shirts. His talent is now primarily in defending this country as a U.S. Marine, and he is nearly a third of the way through a career in that branch of the military. A shooter shoots. A protector protects.

As parents we may have preconceived notions of what we'd like to see our child excel in, envisioning which captains of industry they might be. Yet, ultimately, we're not calling the shots for their future, adult endeavors; they are. We can and should support the ancillary dedication, aptitudes and desires of our offspring. Their particular passion may just be the making of them. And of you.

A parent parents. That's *our* fervor.

Picking your Battles

On any given day, one of my children will announce something or do something ridiculous.

"Mom, I'm going to buy a house when I graduate in May."

"Mommy! I'm going outside!" (And it's raining.)

"Hey, mom. I need a new Ipod. *Now.*"

My daughter, Janet, leaves for school in 40-degree weather in capri pants, a tee-shirt and flip-flops.

As I began to write this, my husband called me into the kitchen to look through the window at Jack, now nine. He had pulled his "pitch back" net under the basketball hoop and was standing on top of it, with his body through the hoop! Stuck.

I wait for the words, "April Fool!" But they do not come, whether it's the first of April or not. It is then that I have to choose in a millisecond whether to look foolish myself by having a tantrum about what was said or done, or take the road less traveled and let the dervishes whirl. Picking battles is not fun, but it's part and parcel of being a parent.

Since there are battles to pick, you would think someone would have shipped me off to parent boot camp during my first pregnancy, but no, it's on-the-mission training. Luckily, by now—nearly 22 years into this battleground—I think I may have reached the rank of Major. I'd love to be the General, but my troops slip me up too often. War is hell.

Although the battles to pick begin even when your child is a toddler, they really increase in intensity and number when your child reaches age 12, and it doesn't let up until 18. (Note that I use the phrase "doesn't let up;" I don't say it stops.) It is the pre-teen and teen years that present the most enemies—hormones, peers, sex, drugs and rock 'n roll.

An adolescent daughter, I am discovering to my horror, is much more of a challenge than an adolescent son. The sleepover curfews; pasting magazine pictures of actors and musical idols all over her walls; the math tests not studied for; the non-weather-appropriate clothing; the non-weather-appropriate clothing that must be purchased at Abercrombie and no place else, and the non-weather-appropriate clothing tossed hither and thither all over her bedroom floor. There's the boyfriend factor; the shoes of mine that go missing; the earrings of mine that also go missing; the hairbrush she borrows from her father and doesn't return causing major commotion each morning. Plus the refusal to take the school bus, and etcetera, etcetera. It is a major command post being the mother of a daughter.

My husband isn't very good about picking his battles, but fortunately, he has Major Julie to remind him about what's important to sweat about and what is simply a matter for gritted teeth.

Example: Kenny wanted to dye his hair blue when he was age 15. Jon hit the roof and yelled at him. I said to let him dye it; he'd have to deal with the consequences of looking like an idiot at school. The next day, however, Kenny dyed Jack's hair blue (Jack was only four years old). That action required big consequences from us, even though Jack grinned like the blue-haired monkey he momentarily was while Kenny sulked.

Choosing which battle to fight is important for both you and your child. If your kindergartner wants to wear his Batman costume to school, let him. His friends will quickly help him decide the choice wasn't brilliant; you won't be the bad guy. If your teenage daughter repeatedly lies about her whereabouts on the weekends, throw her in the brig for a while (but don't throw out your love for her as a person). When your 20-year-old believes he can afford to live in an apartment without the benefit of a steady job, let him try it, but remain ready to provide backup if he calls it in.

Children need to fail, to fall, to embarrass themselves, to experiment. Parents need to be there to catch them, to caution them, to intervene when presented with real health-threatening experiments; to remind them that they are loved. There are skirmishes and then there are ongoing battles. We have to learn when to "send in the Marines," and when to let it go. It doesn't mean that we accept the unacceptable, but we discover the difference between saving our sanity and letting their insanity run its course.

Now, if you'll excuse me, we need to pry our son out from his basketball hoop. And probably laugh this one off.

Parents: Just Say "No"

If you remember being a teenager, then you'll remember how many things you tried to pull off without being caught by your parents or—heaven forbid—the police. These things included, but were not limited to, smoking, drinking, drugging and canoodling with the opposite sex.

It has been said that our generation of parents have tried to be more friend than foe with our children. Guilty as charged on some accounts. My head was more in the sand then out with my two older ones, but only up to a point. Around the time that Kenny turned 14, I suddenly chucked friendly mode for Gestapo.

If he would announce his intentions to go to a party, or even just that he wanted to go to a friend's house after school, I would call the home of his proposed friend appointment to make sure an adult would be present. This would cause major embarrassment and much sulking on his part. But I'm not naive. I keenly remember what I was doing at that age; hanging out in a parentless dwelling was Nirvana. I wouldn't have the sins of the mother (or father or stepfather for that matter) visited on the son.

This is not to imply that he wasn't successful on occasion. If one wants what one wants they'll get it somehow. But, I tried my best, even through his senior year in high school, to remind him about rules, responsibility and the rage of a mother nearly-fooled.

I now have to be Rambo-mom to Janet. Technically, eighth grade was a very long time ago for me, and yet, having a 13-year-old daughter keeps it quite green. She hosted a party recently, and I probably made my presence known to her guests more than I should have, but as I said, she keeps my memory sharp.

Of course, there will be a time when even the good kid is in the wrong place at the wrong time, or that they will inevitably make the off-center decision. As we have done as parents since toddler hood, we can assure them that we will be there should they fall, even if a consequence needs to be handed down.

We have to learn to say "no" early on. "No" to the trip to the toy store; to the third play date of the week; to the ice cream, and to the extra half hour before bed. Then it's "no" to the second sleepover of the weekend, or to wandering aimlessly around downtown; to constant IM-ing; or chauffeuring to and from movies in other towns every weekend. And "no" to unchaperoned gatherings at friends' homes.

For first time parents of teens, navigating the whole stretch of teenage years can be fraught with fog and stormy seas. Yet having made the treacherous journey twice already, I can report that eventually the water calms and the sun shines once again.

But just for the record—and previous teen parenting experience aside—I am so not psyched about doing it all again, two more times. There's not enough grey hair-hiding coloring in the world!

Do Your Kids Make You Proud?

My children complain that I tend to malign them too often in print. That is not my intention, of course, and I hope that interpretation is due to familial sensitivity. Although the kids and their exploits are seemingly an endless source of tongue-in-cheek, as well as serious topic inspiration, they are also the supply of oceans of pride.

Jack and I recently went to see the "American Idols" in concert. This year's winner, Taylor Hicks, dedicated his song, "Do I Make You Proud?" to all those serving in the military around the world. I immediately welled up and Jack gently took my hand, squeezed it and smiled up at me. I was proud on two levels—for Blake due to the obvious, motherly and patriotic reasons—and for Jack because of his maturity and protective instincts.

Of course our children make us proud. And, naturally, we may not always show that support to them as often as we may imagine. Somehow and sometimes the need to correct, to question, to challenge, comes spewing out of us. There is the verbal disclaimer of which we aren't even conscious: "That was a great hit, but …;" "Well a B-plus is fine, but …;" "Thank you for saying 'thank you,' but …;" "Wouldn't you be happier at this college?" or, "I know you tried your best, but …"

To provide some balance here, I offer up a few moments of pride for my four babies. I think it will get your own wheels whirling regarding *your* child's shining moments.

With Jack, many "wow!" moments involve sporting events: Jack intercepting the football and running 20 yards for a touchdown; a game winning catch in center field; sprinting to the top of a portable rock climbing wall. He's also solved puzzles that stump an adult and shoveled snow without being asked or even expected to be asked. He saves every penny of allowance, holiday money and birthday checks.

Janet gave me goose bumps in elementary school when she and a friend sang and danced in the annual variety show, bringing down the house. Three summers ago she roped a calf at her camp's final rodeo, and although seeing a tiny spider will cause her panic, she nevertheless rides horses in the Grand

Tetons amongst black bears. Janet amazes me when she runs to a friend's aid, either literally or via phone or email; her loyalty can be fierce. And her creative writing is inspiring.

Kenny had many a basketball game-saving dunk or three-pointer, the show-stopping lead in a middle school musical, and the ability to solve a Rubik's cube blindfolded in less than three minutes in a talent show. He was valedictorian of his recording arts college class and gave the commencement speech during his entertainment business graduation. And currently he is hoping to launch an online music source. His entrepreneurial side gives me more pride than pause.

As a child, Blake dove into a pool in the cool of late October to save a frog that was headed toward certain death-by-pool-filter. An accomplished artist in high school, he often had his drawings on display in the lobby. He will defend me and protect me emotionally when push comes to shove. And I needn't go into his courage, bravery and commitment as a member of the United States Marine Corps.

Gaining and maintaining self-esteem is a tricky entity with children, adolescents and young adults. Reminding our kids of their worth, of our pride, of how terrific they are even when they may stumble is crucial. So they strike out; big deal. Or they find a "C' on their report card; encourage them anyway.

Catch them doing something good every now and again. It's always happening.

Wrangling the "What Ifs"

All of us—parents or non-parents—suffer in varying degrees from the "What Ifs:" What If my plane crashes? What If I don't get that job? What If I never get married? What If there's no butter at the store?

But once you become a parent—actually before you even meet the apple of your eye—the What Ifs intensify. It all begins with the sobering thought, "What If I'm not ready to be a parent?"

Who is ever totally ready, really? For the responsibility, the sleep deprivation, the aggravation, the love that swells to bursting, and the worrying. Those nagging, insane, trivial and terrifying What Ifs? But ready-or-not, the child comes along with everything listed above, and it is up to us parents, new and not-so-much, to determine which What Ifs are worth losing some hair over, and which are quite simply beyond our control or not worth another sleepless night.

I have suffered, chin-upped and chocolate-powered my way through some pretty legitimate What Ifs, but at the same time I gave the What Ifs more power than they deserved. The most obvious of these was: "What If Blake gets wounded or killed in Iraq?" I would watch and hear the reports of casualties or bloody confrontations and my imagination went whirling into overdrive. It's happened twice and is scheduled to happen again in the fall. "What If I can't do it a third time?" I ask myself. "What If it's worse?" And yet, with each of his deployments, I realize that dwelling on the things I cannot change is futile. I am still playing the tapes, even now, and wondering if I will be able to fully concentrate on my position in the PTC; my responsibilities for a disease fund-raiser; writing this column; Janet and Jack and Jon.

My second oldest son, Kenny, lives in Queens and works in Manhattan. We usually speak on the phone two or three times a week. Last week, I hadn't heard from him and kept getting his voicemail. I heard on the radio that there were subway stabbings on the line that he uses to get to and from the city. I went straight to: "He's in some hospital unconscious or worse and since his last name is different from mine nobody knows to contact me!" I left more frantic voicemails. He called me the next morning.

"Jeez, mom! Every crime that is committed in New York City does not involve me as the victim, just as every Marine killed in Iraq is not Blake!" I laughed at his observations while at the same time remarking, "But you're not a mom!"

Some of the parental What Ifs are just not reality-based, nor should they even merit the strength of their contemplation.

There is a prayer said in certain circles that never fails to ground me when these wild feelings threaten to consume an otherwise sensible mind. It is called the Serenity Prayer: "Grant me the serenity to accept the things I cannot change, the courage to change the things I can, and the wisdom to know the difference." It's a great assemblage of words to remember and repeat whether you are a recovering whatever or not. Anyone can and frankly, *should*, use it when times get tough and perplexing parental thoughts run amuck.

I cannot change our government's policies nor should I challenge Blake's choice of career. I cannot, could not, change the fact that Jack's baseball team didn't make enough hits to win. I cannot change the stone landscape of our pool; instead I have to trust that the kids won't be too foolish and slam their heads onto it. If they do, well, the hospital isn't too far away. I cannot change the fact that the grocery store may be out of butter, but I can adjust and make another choice.

Parents can choose to be paranoid or they can change the level of their anxiety accordingly. We love our children fiercely, passionately desiring to shelter them from storm or pain or humiliation or confusion. But there is always courage and wisdom in changing the "What If (negative thought)" to "What If (positive thought)."

What If you tried that today?

Hellos and Goodbyes

Some of the sweetest, saddest and most sobering moments as a parent can come with hellos and goodbyes with our children. Whether it's an extended separation or a weekend apart, absences conjure up all variety of emotions.

Schools are nearly out for the summer and for some of us that means sleep-away camp for our child or children. For first time campers and their parents the goodbyes can be a potentially teary affair.

Three years ago, Janet went off to her first year at a month-long ranch camp out in Wyoming. Jon and I kept our counsel at the gate, trying not to hug her too hard or appear as apprehensive as all three of us felt. She said her goodbye tentatively and bravely, without looking back as she headed away to her plane. With her out of sight I could then weep, both in excitement for her adventure and that motherly fear of the unknown for her child.

The hello at the end of those four weeks was wonderful. As soon as she spotted us on final rodeo/pick-up day, she ran fast towards us, plaited hair flying as her cowboy boots kicked up small dust clouds around her bluejeaned legs. She seemed taller, and the sprinkling of freckles across her nose and cheeks made her look more beautiful than ever. She grabbed me in the tightest embrace of her young life and both of us dissolved into happy tears. Each year since that greeting is repeated with no less intensity, even if the goodbye has gotten easier.

Jack will be heading off to that same camp's boys session next week and I am anticipating a harder parting of the ways in the wee morning hours at JFK. Perhaps it is because he is my baby? I am not sure, but I will need to keep my tears in check with the same painful force that I employ every time I have to say goodbye to Blake when he heads back to his base or off to a deployment.

Crying with Jack is likely to set him off. Crying with Blake may set him off, but in a different way. I can't let him see me sweat; weakness is not an option in his presence. Until I say hello again.

This coming Sunday morning he arrives home from his third deployment, and like the other two before, we both know I will break down. I will hug him as firmly as Janet did me after that first summer at camp, and I don't care if he is embarrassed or secretly overcome himself. I cry out of my forced courage endured over the past nine months.

My hellos and goodbyes with Kenny are easy and joyful on both accounts. Although he and I were both apprehensive when he initially journeyed off to college in Florida, the excitement over what was to come was palatable. He has been living in Queens since graduation two years ago, Metro North-ing back home at least once a month. We both smile broadly and assuredly upon arrival and departure. Soon, however, he is embarking on a many months-long cross country trek, and I am fairly certain that particular goodbye will choke me up.

Whether our child is hopping on the school bus for the first time or climbing aboard an airplane that will take him thousands of miles away, the parting is such sweet sorrow. It is an opportunity for growth for both parties; the change is etched in stone.

Remember this: our love travels with them both until and after the return.

·

Waiting to Exhale

The nature of the business of being parents means that we must often endure, wait out, and try to help when our child is caught up in the grip of emotional, social or physical pain. We gasp, we hold our breath, we pray, and we wait to exhale.

Our child may be diagnosed with a disease, an illness or an injury. After doing all that we can possibly do to support them and aid in their recovery, often the results are left in the hands of those more knowledgeable, or in something/someone greater than ourselves. Many times it is up to our child to help themselves, and it is the waiting for that to happen which takes our breath away. The expression, "time takes time," is both a balm and bewilderment.

A child may impulsively quit their job with no prospects on the horizon. They may decide high school isn't for them and we watch as their grades plummet. An undiagnosed learning disability derails our eight-year-old. As mothers and fathers of teens we pretty much have to inhale and suck it up for two, three, four years, especially if teenaged angst makes them implode. In preschool or in elementary school our child may be one of the bullies or the bullied, and we wait both patiently and impatiently for this too to pass. A son goes to war and the anxiety is unbearable at times, yet bear it we must.

Blake has been deployed since last September, and was in Iraq for the last five months. We learned late last week that he had arrived in Kuwait. He will be there for a couple of weeks until the naval ship arrives to begin the journey of bringing the Marines and Sailors stateside. And so on that score I have begun the exhaling process, which isn't fully complete until I can wrap my arms around the big lug sometime in June.

During a shopping trip to the local sporting goods store this week, I received a hug from the owner, who is also a friend, upon hearing the news of Blake's exit from Iraq. He commented on my big smile and the look of relief in my face.

"Yes," I beamed, for the first time in a long time. "The breathing out is welcome."

We all want our children safe, sane and secure. When bad or uncomfortable news visits our child, we must hang onto hope—that the cancer will go into remission; that the ADD will become under control; that he can play ball again or that her leg will heal enough so may she dance once more. We pray that their heart will mend or that their lost soul will be found; that their disability won't impede success; or that self-destructive behaviors can morph back into self-love, or that combat will not offer the ultimate sacrifice. As tempting as it is for us to run for the bedcovers or self-medicate, we must remember that what is happening is happening more to *them* than to us. We need to get out of our own way and try to be present for our child.

That feeling a mother gets as she watches her five-year-old first board that big yellow bus for kindergarten is repeated over and over as the child ages. It's the "Omigosh-omigosh-are-they-going-to-be-okay?" mini panic attack; the big intake of air, the flutters in the belly, and the pounding of the heart so full of love it hurts.

Holding on to hope is the tool we can use when these moments present themselves (and they will). Hope and choice: Will we let this situation crush us or our child, or will we choose to gain new strength and perspective? Will we inhale so tightly that we can never again breathe easily?

Carl Jung once said, "I am not what happened to me; I am what I choose to become." That is a lesson, a mantra, that we can teach our children and also, of course, ourselves when the chips are down.

Breathe, baby. Just breathe.

12
PARENTING 20-SOMETHINGS

Temporarily Re-Feathering the Nest

For the past two years, I have had a half-empty (or half-full) nest. Blake has been away with the Marine Corps for four years, and when Kenny graduated from high school, he moved down to Winter Park, Florida for two years of media arts college. The "big boys" were gone and the younger two, Janet and Jack remained.

I missed my big boys. The house felt strange without their presence and, of course, so whole again when they would visit. And both Kenny and I assumed that upon his graduation this spring, he would get an apartment in New York City. Last fall, I declared our house as too big now without the big guys, and so, for that reason and others, we recently moved to a slightly smaller home just miles down the road.

I figured that the new house wouldn't carry as many "ghosts" of Blake and Kenny, since they hadn't lived in it, and maybe I wouldn't miss them as much. Sure, they would visit for holidays, or in Blake's case, duty leave, but when they would go back to their lives, perhaps I wouldn't feel as lonely without them. (Bear in mind that I had been a single parent with them for five years, so our bond is tight.)

But, it turns out, there will be ghosts. Because assumptions have a way of not seeing fruition: two weeks ago, new college grad Kenny moved himself and all of his recording equipment into the spare bedroom above the garage for the summer and fall.

College students and graduates often come home for the summer. Parental curfews and guidelines are temporarily reinstated. We have to keep one ear open again for the sound of a car coming in the driveway in the wee hours. Our refrigerator is over-stocked for the time being, and just as quickly emptied. Teenagers or 20-something's enter our side doors without knocking. As the kids are wont to say, "It's all good."

For the graduate who returns to the nest, it's a bit of a drag to have to live with mom and dad, and maybe a brother or sister or two. Having been living in a dorm or an apartment for the duration of college, it feels awkward not to be as independent (but of course the free room and board is a bonus!).

Before when Blake and Kenny would come home at Christmas or a similar visit, I would remind them not to drink-and-drive, or to call if they were going to be out late, or not come home at all. It's one thing when they are not under my roof; I still worry, but it's not as intimate a worry. When their clothes are strewn on the floor of their room and their favorite cookies are in my cookie jar, I want to know where they are and more or less what they're doing.

"Mom," Blake said last year. "I was in a war. In Iraq. I know what I'm doing. I can handle myself."

"War, shmar." I replied. "I'm your commanding officer right now and I need to know where you are."

Kenny has been great so far. The car is safely in the driveway in the morning. He calls if he is extending his stay in the city with his buddies. And, I love the music he creates, so the loud sounds that occasionally emanate from his room are oddly soothing.

The extra feather in our new nest will fly away again when the late autumn winds blow and I may feel slightly hollow again. But it's all temporary. For right now, I will enjoy having three kids around, because as Kenny pointed out, with him just turning 20 this past weekend, and Janet becoming 12, I will have one year of a teenager-less house.

That's not a bad deal. Even if it is temporary as well.

Back to the "Sandbox"

When my column debuted back in the spring of 2004, my oldest son, Blake, currently a sergeant in the United States Marine Corps, was on his second deployment in Iraq, a place we Marine moms refer to as "the sandbox." As I write this, he is on a naval ship steaming back towards the Middle East theatre for his third combat tour. He has so far not been given clearance to tell me exactly where he will end up.

Some people assume I should be used to this by now. Well-intentioned, they remind me of how terrifically trained Blake is, as though I am somehow unaware of that fact. They tell me this as if somehow these skills will automatically guarantee his return, alive and physically unscathed.

On a bright September morning five years ago, thousands of families said, "See you later, honey," to thousands of husbands, wives, sons, daughters and significant others. They had absolutely no reason to believe that they would not return home, alive, physically, as well as mentally, unharmed. Since then, my son and his brethren have been fighting primarily to avenge those senseless casualties (that is the mindset these warriors must have; they can't politicize). And although Blake is simply going to work as well, he is also most obviously in a danger zone. It is not a run-of-the-mill day at the office.

This is not a tale of woe and please-pity-the-military-parent. I am incredibly proud of my son, and I am far from alone in my fear. There are scores of other anxious parents of those deployed men and women standing in my shoes, just as parents of soldiers, airmen, sailors and Marines have done during other conflicts for decades.

But it is still a lousy position to be in, to worry for a child, who—although he willingly chose this profession months before 9/11—may or may not return to my arms. I think perhaps parents of police officers and firefighters might harbor that exact feeling of trepidation. And then there is the matter of trying to keep it all together for my other children safely ensconced here in our beautiful town.

Don't scream, don't cry, don't take to my bed; I try to do those things while they are out of ear shot or at school. I need to not talk about it as much in their company as I did during his first deployment in 2003. Jack and Kenny continue to take it in stride. Their battling brother is cool and invincible. When Janet gets nervous, a hug can work wonders.

I realize and appreciate that all of this is foreign to many parents, and I am grateful for this indulgence. Sympathy is not what I'm after from other moms and dads, but neither is the occasional assumption that I shouldn't be apprehensive. Just some validation of feeling is all that is requested. The kid is literally in the line of fire and it's not always easy for me to wrap my cranium around that truth.

We all want our children to be safe, whether they're walking down the street, or dashing down a football field, leaping off a balance beam, traveling off to college or riding their tricycle around the driveway. We hope that they will be forever there.

Last autumn, probably as part of my mid-life crisis, or as a nod to my multi-tattooed Marine, I had a small tattoo imprinted on the inside of my ankle of the word "Hope." That word and that concept is what keeps me going. It is what keeps any parent going in the face of frustration, disturbance, illness, or irritation.

And all I hope for my fellow military parents and for myself is a hug. No rationalizations, no disbeliefs that I'm not more "okay" with this. Just a hug, plus a silent salute for those who continue to serve.

My Son, the Hobo

School is beginning next week. Whether your child is entering kindergarten, his senior year of high school or her junior year of college, your thoughts most likely follow this track: "Oh! What will he/she be when they 'grow up'?" Doctor, lawyer, Indian chief?

My son? My 22-year-old son with his valedictorian trimmed Bachelor of Arts? Well, he's a hobo!

According to Kenny, "a *hobo* is defined as a migratory worker who likes to travel, a *tramp* travels without working, and a *bum* does not travel or work." His self-proclaimed "Hobo Lifestyle 2.0" is for enjoying. As he says on his website for the chronicles of this adventure: "I intend to experience as much as I can by traveling. As for work, right now I have some cool ideas I've gotten started on, and none of them require me to physically be somewhere. Perfect. Now it's time to be everywhere ..."

Ah, it's every parent's dream, right? Wait, let me adjust my aneurysm.

The kid had a full-time job for two years after graduation (he earned his B.A. in two years at an intense, year 'round college). He has student loan payments, plus cell phone charges, and had rent, utilities and food to pay for before embarking on the hobo life earlier this summer. He had been making extra money recording demos for musicians out of his apartment in New York. Additionally, he has a teeny wee bit of cash coming in from two separate web businesses which are still not completely up on the scale they need to be for, say, Google to come a 'calling with their billions of dollars.

And now he literally carries his life on his back. There is no plan. It's just a Jack Kerouac kind of escapade.

When I shipped him off to kindergarten 17 years ago, he waved from behind his Teenage Ninja Turtle back pack, his smile big, bold and full of promise. Two weeks ago, I left him at the Whitefish, Montana train depot. He waved goodbye from behind his four-foot-high North Face pack, sleeping bag dangling from the side, with a smile: big, bold and full of promise. I failed miserably at *not* looking miserable, wildly wiping tears off my face, not unlike that clear, cool September morning of his kindergarten inauguration. Oh, for crying out load (literally); why am I letting him just go like that?! The answer: because I really have no choice.

We all need to find ourselves. Many of us do it while struggling through that first pay-your-dues job after high school or college. Some of us don't find ourselves or our professional passion until middle age. And a few of us—like Kenny—need to literally travel in and around ourselves and our surroundings to hit upon our essence.

The good news? He has a decent and solid education under his frayed, hobo belt; he was born with a keen intelligence and a craftily creative streak. The local school systems laid the foundation and the basics. Now nature will take its course.

Our kids can be anything they want to be and sometimes what we guide them towards as well. As they board that school bus next week, please know that their journey will actually go beyond Easy-readers and fractions and colonial times and chemistry. We and their teachers are the conduits on their educational, professional, social and personal quest.

And because it can be a survival of the fittest, I suggest packing them a can of bear mace, too. Kenny has his at the ready.

Whose House is it, Anyway?

Older children grow and go on their merry way. But inevitably they come back—during Christmas break, the occasional long weekend here and there, and of course, summer vacation. My Marine is home maybe once a year, but he still leaves his mark. They all do.

It's a wonderful thing having your college-aged and older kids come home. But, after the first day or so, you begin to feel the tilt in your daily routine. There are more dishes to wash, more laundry to fold, more food to buy. At night, when they are out and about, there is the waiting to hear the garage door open and close, or for the sound of heavy footsteps in the kitchen at three in the morning. Sounds you haven't had to worry about in months. Sounds I know I shouldn't be listening for, and yet I can't help myself. Blake has been in combat in Iraq twice and Kenny has been living in an apartment while attending college in Florida, but while they are under my roof, I worry myself silly. What if they get hurt? What if they drink and drive? And then I get annoyed both at myself for worrying and for them for staying out until who-knows-when.

I have a good friend who this past week had her boarding school junior and his college-aged sister home. "I can't stand it!" she cried. "I just lost it on them last night and locked myself in my room!" For days she complained of their sleeping in until noon, of the mess left in the kitchen, and of late nights out, all amongst the chaos of Christmas. She loves them dearly and was looking forward to having them home. But sometimes the reality is quite different from the Norman Rockwellian picture in our mind.

It's an odd feeling. I can't wait to have the big boys home. I pray for it and I plan for it, and then I'm overwhelmed by the enormity of it all. Blake bringing home huge containers of protein powders that line my counter-tops. Kenny leaving empty Capris Sun pouches everywhere like Easter eggs that I discover months later on bookcases and on ceiling beams. The scent of dirty socks emanating from their bedroom. Large, lanky and loud friends walking in and out of our house. Friends I am pleased to see, but friends I am not prepared to greet sporting bed-head and pajamas. I am happy to have a fuller and busier home. But I am also secretly glad that it's only for a finite amount of time. At least I think I am secretly glad.

What can I say? The house is crazy when full, and I have a love-hate relationship with it. Yet when it is *half* full, I ache for Kenny or Blake's invasion.

Whose House is it, Anyway? It's ours, it's theirs. It's love.

13
WHEN YOU'RE YOUNG AT HEART

Embarrassing Our Offspring

Kids have been embarrassed by their parents forever, especially teenagers.

From the time I hit age 11 I was prone to the whiny-phrased, "Daaaadddy! You're embarrassing me!" He would shimmy and shake in public to the music of the Supremes and Crystal Gale, and an assortment of other 1960's-1970's recording industry artists. He was also prone to calling me "Baby Julie" in front of my friends. There were an array of other awkward moments, some real and many, in all probability, imagined.

The other night I took Janet up to Hartford to attend the popular phenomenon "High School Musical" in concert. As the first song burst into life a mere four rows in front of us, I began to sway my arms back and forth with the rest of the audience. In a flash she was slapping my arms down. "You are *not* allowed to do that, mom. No!" Anytime I began to clap or try to move my body to the infectious rhythms I was met with a determined and deadly look that clearly translated to: "Do not embarrass me."

It's fun though.

When Kenny and Blake were in middle school I apparently mortified them as they played in basketball games by shouting their names, followed by the supportive words "Yay!", "Go!" and "Alright!" They told me in no uncertain terms that I was to sit on my hands and zip my lip. I mostly obeyed their edict, but occasionally I would let the enthusiasm fly if for no other reason than to watch them wince or squirm. Jack has taken over where they left off, yet since he's only 10 he seems to be cutting me some slack.

My sense of fashion now and again is a deep well of embarrassment for not only my daughter but also for my sons. And I love it. "What are you *wearing*?!" can leap from all four of their lips. Of course, their sense of fashion has embarrassed *me* on occasion. Take the mid-to-late '90s, when Blake and Kenny insisted on wearing these baggy jeans half way across their nether regions so that one could eyeball the tops to the midway of their boxers. Even when wearing dress shirts their khakis would sit casually at their hips, the hint of undergarments peaking out from atop their waistbands.

I wear my ability to embarrass like a badge of honor. To me, it means I am doing my job. My biggest stunt to date? Last Christmas, for our annual holiday party, I came downstairs wearing the following get-up: A "Sexy Santa" costume. It was a low-cut, short red dress trimmed in white fur, black fish net stockings, boots and accessorized with red satin gloves also with white trim. Not only did my husband have a coronary, but my kids either screamed in horror (Janet), laughed (Jack) or shook their heads, turned pink and denied I was their mother (Blake and Kenny). All five members of my family requested that I change my attire.

No way. I was 49 years old at the time and I reserved the right to do as I pleased; I'd earned it. And guess what? All the men at the party appreciated the look, the women laughed unthreatened, and I am hoping that my husband felt embarrassed for not cherishing the look more.

And there's nothing embarrassing about realizing one can still turn a male head or two, four decades and four children later.

Explaining Midlife "Crisis" To the Kids

Somewhere between the ages of 40 to 50-plus, something subtle or not-so-subtle occurs in all of us. Maybe it's a throwback to teenage rebellion, or perhaps it's a determination to try something new or daring; to break free from perceived or actual restraints. At midlife, we take a step back, look behind and attempt a peek at what's ahead. And while we're doing this, our children may or may not take notice.

Not all of us have this midlife "crisis," and I put it in quotes because the word conjures up such drama. But many of us do experience a change or a life-altering choice. We consider chucking the corporate world to farm (or vise versa), to the stereotypical sports car and an affair, to living so stupendously healthy and fit that our friends become envious. We may choose to cut our hair really short and wear bright red whenever possible.

Or, take our case for example.

Since my husband, Jon, turned 40, he's run three marathons in as many years, and began attending rock concerts with his friends and business associates with much of the fervor he once employed as a 20-something. He'll absolutely kill me if I name the bands, but I will offer these hints: most are groups that 29-year-olds follow or that were popular some 29 years ago.

"Where's daddy?" Jack will ask in the evening about every four to eight weeks.

"At a concert," I'll answer and name the band. "He'll be home tomorrow night."

Janet will roll her eyes. What comes out of her mouth next isn't a curse word, but it still borders on the disrespectful in its tone of disbelief. Maybe it's hard for her to imagine her dad rocking out in his business suit (even though I know he changes into jeans).

Concerts, running long distances and ogling sports cars beats some of the alternatives. I too, can be baffling to Jack and Janet, as well as Kenny and Blake, and probably Jon as well.

A few years into my 40's I decided, a propos of perhaps nothing, that the family had to move out of Weston. Now. And so, three months later, we were living here in New Canaan.

"Why do we have to move?" Blake had asked, then a high school junior determined to graduate from Weston High.

"Because," I answered, simply. A woman of a certain age shouldn't have to explain in great deal, even to her own child. Of course, "because" was pretty much all I could come up with to explain it to myself!

I also began to dress a bit funkier—not always, but sometimes. Maybe it's a child of the early '70s thing. I made a decision to dress as I feel comfortable and not for conformity to a particular community. There have been numerous moments over the past decade where my kids have looked at my chosen outfit and exclaimed that I need to change, or that I am embarrassing them. Or as Janet and Blake so succinctly put it, "*No* mom! No," as they shake their head in bewilderment.

This past summer I paraglided from 11,000 feet off of the Jackson Hole ski mountain. And my most recent indulgence into midlife mania is a red Mustang convertible, not unlike the one I drove during high school in the 1970's. The face in the rear-view mirror is age 17; don't attempt to tell me differently. I even secured the same vanity license plates that I had back then: "JUBUT." This has really rocked my family's world.

"But you're not Julie Butler anymore," they said, especially the members of the family with the "Evans" last name. Blake and Kenny (Flannery) are equally as bemused, of course.

"Of course I am!" I exclaim. "I will always be Julie Butler! 'Evans' is also my name, but I will never *not* be a 'Butler!'"

Back away from the madwoman.

And so off I drive, hair flying, face flashing a big smile, Carole King blaring from the speakers; a midlife "crisis" in motion.

The kids, the husband, wonder where mom went, yet they know I'm still here, still there. I'm just cruising the crisis in style.

14
AND IN THE END ...

Does it get any Easier?!

I don't think it matters whether you have one child or a dozen, at some point—or at many points—you are going to wonder aloud, "How old do the kids have to be before raising them gets any easier?"

I don't have an answer and I have four of the suckers, ages 12 to 24. So one would think I might have some sage advice. And yet, I don't. Certain ages seem easier to negotiate than others, but crucial mitigating factors sneak in there, and one mother's easy is another mother's walking, talking nightmare. Not comforting, I know.

I was recently moaning over the telephone to my sister-in-law out in Wyoming about some teenage trial or other. She said to me, "Well, Julie, it's not your first time at the rodeo." One doesn't have to be from a western mountain state to fully appreciate that statement. And it's a pretty great one, isn't it? *"Not your first time at the rodeo"* is now taped to my computer. Perhaps it will become a new mantra. And when I say it, I picture myself as either the rodeo clown—dodging and weaving and being laughed at—or as one of those fairly confident looking, really cool, fringy and fuzzy chaps-wearing cowboys sitting high and solid aboard a bucking bronc. I'm twirling my hat around my head, yee-hawing, just before I am catapulted off and up and head-first into manure.

I would have to say that the teen years are the hardest, the most challenging, but that statement seems a no-brainer. With hormones and identity-searching raging, being a teenager and *raising* a teenager is fraught with conflict and confusion. Yet as stated earlier, mitigating factors can make the teen years either a piece of cake or a piece of scat. It's in the "lap of the gods," as my late, great mom used to say.

The middle school years aren't a walk in the park either, and my fourth and final child is right smack in the, well, *middle* of them. Even though it's a been-there-done-that thing, I can nonetheless occasionally be discovered curled up in the fetal position wailing: "Does it get any easier?" By now one would think I'd know the answer. I do, I do know the answer, and it is: "Not yet." Although, to be fair, Jack is hands-down the easiest child I have had to raise, but at only 12, there's still plenty of time to terrorize. I need to be cautious not to become too complacent ... he can execute a sneak attack at any moment.

"I couldn't hit a wall with a six gun, but I can twirl one. It looks good."

John Wayne

While raising children doesn't truly get any easier, I can at least try and look as if I'm doing it in a fairly effortless manner. You know, "act as if ..." Act as if I know exactly what to do when a tantrum presents itself; or a kid forgets to phone on Mother's Day; or a son doesn't feel like working full-time; a daughter doesn't realize the meaning or purpose of a clothes hanger, or a sixth grader insists that his bedtime can be just as late as a ninth grader's. Act as if I don't long to escape to my own private island, sans everybody and anything but some sunscreen.

In the end, I suppose *easy* isn't interesting. This makes my life quite the rodeo indeed.

Printed in the United States
205627BV00002B/1-123/P

9 780595 488957